Understanding
Web Development

ISBN 0-13-025844-X

9 780130 258441

90000

THE FOUNDATIONS OF WEB SITE ARCHITECTURE SERIES

AVAILABLE DECEMBER 1999

UNDERSTANDING WEB DEVELOPMENT
Arlyn Hubbell, *Merrimack College*

ADMINISTRATING WEB SERVERS, SECURITY & MAINTENANCE
Eric Larson, *Sun Microsystems & Merrimack College*
Brian Stephens, *Sun Microsystems & Merrimack College*

EXPLORING WEB MARKETING & PROJECT MANAGEMENT
Donald Emerick, *Merrimack College & WOW*
Kimberlee Round, *Merrimack College & Surf's Up Web Development*
Susan Joyce

COMING SPRING 2000

CREATING WEB GRAPHICS, AUDIO & VIDEO
Mike Mosher

COMING SPRING 2000
THE ADVANCED WEB SITE ARCHITECTURE SERIES

DESIGNING WEB INTERFACES, HYPERTEXT & MULTIMEDIA
Michael Rees, *Bond University*
Andrew White, *FirstTech Computer*
Bebo White, *Stanford Linear Accelerator Center, Stanford University*

SUPPORTING WEB SERVERS, NETWORKING, PROGRAMMING, & EMERGING TECHNOLOGIES
Joseph Silverman, *UCSF Stanford Health Care*
Michael Wendling, *@Home Network*
Bebo White, *Stanford Linear Accelerator Center, Stanford University*

EXPLORING ELECTRONIC COMMERCE, SITE MANAGEMENT, & INTERNET LAW
Dianne Brinson, *Ladera Press*
Benay Dara-Abrams, *Dara-Abrams Ventures*
Kathryn Henniss, *HighWire Press, Stanford University*
Jennifer Masek, *Stanford Linear Accelerator Center, Stanford University*
Ruth McDunn, *Stanford Linear Accelerator Center, Stanford University*
Bebo White, *Stanford Linear Accelerator Center, Stanford University*

Understanding
Web Development

Arlyn Hubbell

Prentice Hall PTR
Upper Saddle River, NJ 07458
www.phptr.com

Editorial/production supervision: *Kathleen M. Caren*
Acquisitions editor: *Karen McLean*
Editorial assistant: *Michael Fredette*
Manufacturing manager: *Alexis R. Heydt*
Marketing manager: *Kate Hargett*
Cover design director: *Jerry Votta*
Interior designer: *Meryl Poweski*

 © 2000 Prentice Hall PTR
Prentice-Hall, Inc.
Upper Saddle River, NJ 07458

Prentice Hall books are widely used by corporations and government agencies for training, marketing, and resale.

The publisher offers discounts on this book when ordered in bulk quantities. For more information, contact: Corporate Sales Department, Phone: 800-382-3419; Fax: 201-236-7141; E-mail: corpsales@prenhall.com; or write: Prentice Hall PTR, Corp. Sales Dept., One Lake Street, Upper Saddle River, NJ 07458.

All products or services mentioned in this book are the trademarks or service marks of their respective companies or organizations.

ISBN 0-13-025844-X

Prentice-Hall International (UK) Limited, *London*
Prentice-Hall of Australia Pty. Limited, *Sydney*
Prentice-Hall Canada Inc., *Toronto*
Prentice-Hall Hispanoamericana, S.A., *Mexico*
Prentice-Hall of India Private Limited, *New Delhi*
Prentice-Hall of Japan, Inc., *Tokyo*
Pearson Education Asia Pte. Ltd.
Editora Prentice-Hall do Brasil, Ltda., *Rio de Janeiro*

DEDICATION

This is dedicated to:

My students, without whom I'd never have learned to teach

and

My teachers, without whom I'd never have learned to learn.

CONTENTS

FROM THE EDITOR

As the Internet rapidly becomes the primary commerce and communications medium for virtually every company and organization operating today, a growing need exists for trained individuals to manage this medium. Aptly named Webmasters, these individuals will play leading roles in driving their organizations into the next millennium.

Working with the World Organization of Webmasters (WOW), Prentice Hall PTR has developed two book series that are designed to train Webmasters to meet this challenge. These are the Foundations of Website Architecture Series, and the Advanced Website Architecture Series.

The goal of the Foundations of Website Architecture Series is to provide a complete, entry-level Webmaster training curriculum. This series is designed to introduce and explain the technical, business and content management skills that are necessary to effectively train the new Webmaster.

Books in the Foundations of Website Architecture Series include:

Understanding Web Development,

Administrating Web Servers, Security and Maintenance,

Exploring Web Marketing and Project Management,

Creating Web Graphics, Audio and Video.

The Webmaster who grasps the materials in these books will:

- be able to build and maintain static Web sites with limited database-enabled and interactive functionality
- have a working knowledge of server administration, multimedia technologies, and security issues
- be able to interface with IT and content development professionals on these topics
- understand the basics of Web marketing and effective communication
- learn how to manage the creation and construction of Web sites

- manage teams of professionals responsible for Web communication
- achieve a firm understanding of the various Web technologies.

The Advanced Website Architecture Series offers more in-depth coverage of the content, business and technical issues that challenge Webmasters. Books in this series are:

Designing Web Interfaces, Hypertext and Multimedia,

Supporting Web Servers, Networking, Programming, and Emerging Technologies,

Exploring Electronic-Commerce, Site Management, and Internet Law

Thank you for your interest in the Foundations of Website Architecture Series, and good luck in your career as a webmaster!

Karen McLean
Senior Editor
Pearson PTR Interactive

EXECUTIVE FOREWORD

Within the next few years, you will think about the Internet in the same way you think about electricity today. Just as you don't ask your companion to "use electricity to turn on a light," you will assume the omnipresence of the Web and the capabilities that it delivers. The Web is transforming the way we live, work, and play, just as electricity changed everything for previous generations.

Every indication suggests that the explosive growth of Web will continue. The question we need to address is "How can we deliver the most value with this ubiquitous resource?" Today, most of the world's Web sites were created and are maintained by self-taught Webmasters. Why? Because there were limited opportunities to receive formal standards-based education. Quality accessible and affordable education will help provide the broad range of knowledge, skills and abilities to meet the demands of the marketplace.

Over the last three years, the World Organization of Webmasters has worked with colleges and universities, business and industry, and its own membership of aspiring and practicing Web professionals to develop the Certified Professional Webmaster (CPW) program. Our three-part goal is to provide:

- educational institutions with guidelines around which to develop curricula.
- students with an organized way to master technical skills, content development proficiency, and personal workplace ability.
- employers with a standard of achievement to assess Webmaster candidates.

The Foundations of Web Site Architecture Series and The Advanced Web Site Architecture Series grew organically from the communities they will serve. Written by working professionals and academics currently teaching the material, reviewed by leading faculty at major universities and the WOW Review Board of industry professionals, and published by Prentice

Hall PTR, these books are designed to meet the increasingly urgent need for Webmasters with expertise in three areas: technical development, design and content development, and business.

Projections indicate greater than 25 million Web sites online worldwide by 2002. Think of these books as state-of-the-art field guides for those who will shape our online future.

Bill

William B. Cullifer
Executive Director-Founder
World Organization of Webmasters
Bill@joinwow.org

ABOUT THE AUTHOR

Arlyn Hubbell has been involved with the Internet since 1979, when she first discovered online real-time conferencing while finishing her senior thesis at Bates College in Maine. After nearly a decade on Wall Street, she returned to Bates in 1989 as a member of Academic Computing Support Services and quickly became involved in training students, faculty, and staff in the use of Internet tools such as email, Usenet, and Gopher. A one year contract at MIT and three years as Manager of Web Support Services at Shore.Net, a regional ISP in MA, solidified her expertise regarding the Web.

She has been an instructor at Merrimack College since 1996, and was involved in the initial development of courses for the College's Webmaster Certificate Program. She still teaches the courses presented here, much to the joy and consternation of students completing the Web composition requirements of the program.

Arlyn currently lives on an island off the coast of Massachusetts, evidence that it is indeed possible to realize lifelong dreams.

INTRODUCTION

The purpose of this book, *Understanding Web Development*, is to help you establish a firm understanding of how to create an effective Web site in UNIX environment. You will learn the fundamentals of setup, design and maintenance through a series of examples and exercises that build on each other and you are encouraged to apply the concepts you learn in each chapter to a project of your own. As you master the techniques and ideas presented, use them to create your own Web pages and combine them in ways that are pleasing to you.

The idea is to learn by doing, and it is hope of the author that the process will be an enjoyable one for you. As you work through the chapters presented here, do not hesitate to question and experiment. Do not be afraid to make mistakes, or do something simply because you like it. While learning the foundations of design and development is essential, it is taking it all one step further and creating your own style that will bring you the most satisfaction.

It is most important, though, to keep in mind that everything is subject to change in the world of Web design. HTML standards change, available technology changes, and tastes change over time. This is likely not the first book about Web design you have looked at and we guarantee it will not be the last if you work in the field. Learning the basics here is only the beginning; you will find that keeping up with all that is latest and greatest is a constant and never-ending process that can often be as frustrating as it is exciting.

Our goal is to provide you with a solid base from which you will be able to proceed in the direction of your choosing.

HOW THIS BOOK IS ORGANIZED

In this book, and the others in this series, you are presented with a series of interactive labs. Each lab begins with Learning Objectives that define what Exercises (or tasks) are covered in that Lab. This is followed by an overview of the concepts that will be further explored through the Exercises, which are the heart of each Lab.

Each Exercise consists of either a series of steps that you will follow to perform a specific task or a presentation of a particular scenario. Questions that are designed to help you discover the important things on your own are then asked of you. The answers to these questions are given at the end of the Exercises, along with more in-depth discussion of the concepts explored.

At the end of each Lab is a series of multiple-choice Self-Review Questions, which are designed to bolster your learning experience by providing opportunities to check your absorption of important material. The answers to these questions appear in Appendix A. There are also additional Self-Review Questions at this book's companion Web site, found at `http://www.phptr.com/phptrinteractive/`.

Finally, at the end of each chapter, you will find a "Test Your Thinking" section, which consists of a series of projects designed to solidify all of the skills you have learned in the chapter. If you have successfully completed all of the Labs in the chapter, you should be able to tackle these projects with few problems. There are not always "answers" to these projects, but where appropriate, you will find guidance and/or solutions at the companion Web site.

The final element of this book actually doesn't appear in the book at all. It is the companion Web site, and it is located at:

`http://www.phptr.com/phptrinteractive/`

This companion Web site is closely integrated with the content of this book, and we encourage you to visit often. It is designed to provide unique interactive online experiences that will enhance your education. As mentioned, you will find guidance and solutions that will help you complete the projects found in the Test Your Thinking section of each chapter.

You will also find additional Self-Review Questions for each chapter, which are meant to give you more opportunities to become familiar with terminology and concepts presented in the publications. In the Author's Corner, you will find additional information that we think will interest you, including updates to the information presented in these publications, and discussion about the constantly changing technology in which Webmasters must stay involved.

Finally, you will find a Message Board, which you can think of as a virtual study lounge. Here, you can interact with other *Foundations of Website Architecture Series* readers, share and discuss your projects.

NOTES TO THE STUDENT

This publication and the others in the Website Architecture series are endorsed by the World Organization of Webmasters. The series is a training curriculum designed to provide aspiring Webmasters with the skills they need to perform in the marketplace. The skill sets included in the Website Architecture series were initially collected and defined by this international trade association to create a set of core competencies for students, professionals, trainers, and employers to utilize.

NOTES TO THE INSTRUCTOR

Chances are that you are a pioneer in the education field whether you want to be one or not. Due to the explosive nature of the Internet's growth, very few Webmaster training programs are currently in existence. But as you read this, many colleges, community colleges, technical institutes, corporate and commercial training environments are introducing this material into curriculums worldwide.

Chances are, however, that you are instructing new material in a new program. But don't fret, this publication and series are designed as a comprehensive introductory curriculum in this field. Students successfully completing this program of study will be fully prepared to assume the responsibilities of a Webmaster in the field or to engage in further training and certification the Internet communications field.

Each chapter in this book is broken down into sections. All questions and projects have the answers and discussions associated with them. The Labs and question/answer formats used in this book provide excellent opportunities for group discussions and dialogue between students, instructors, and each other. In addition, many answers and their discussions are abbreviated in this publication due to space constraints. Any comments, ideas or suggestions to this text and series will be would be greatly appreciated.

CHAPTER 1

A WEBMASTER'S INTRODUCTION TO UNIX

 Classic. A book which people praise and don't read.

Samuel Langhorn Clemens
Pudd'nhead Wilson (1864)
Pudd'nhead Wilson's Calendar, Ch. 16

CHAPTER OBJECTIVES

In this chapter, you will learn about:

✔ Why it is important to be conversant with
   the UNIX operating system   Page 2
✔ Logging in to a UNIX host via the FTP and telnet
   protocols   Page 4
✔ Basic UNIX commands   Page 11
✔ File and directory management   Page 17
✔ File and directory permissions   Page 24

While the UNIX operating system is ancient by Internet standards, a few years shy of 30 years old at this writing[1], it is still the foundation of the Internet and warrants some serious attention. In an online world that has become cluttered with point-and-click, UNIX is a blessed relief to the harried Webmaster who wants to make a simple, immediate change. Once mastered at almost any level, UNIX is indeed the classic of the Internet. Not only does it serve as the cleanest and most efficient means of accomplishing many tasks, but a solid understanding of the system will allow you to progress more confidently into the areas of Web and system administration in the future. It requires a small amount of effort to learn if you have no previous experience with a command-line operating environment, but you will appreciate it in the end. As most students have found, you may hate it now, but you will love it later.

SELECTING YOUR LOGIN ID AND PASSWORD

To do the exercises and projects in this workbook, you will need a shell account on a UNIX machine running the Apache Web server. This can be acquired from many ISPs,[2] and in most cases, is not terribly expensive. During the process of setting up your account, you will be asked to select a login ID and then, in most cases, be assigned a password.

Your login ID identifies who you are to the computer and must be unique. Many people like to use some variation of their name for this purpose, depending on what is available on the host machine.

A password is, in essence, the key to your account. In the UNIX environment, it is six to eight characters in length and should contain a combination of upper- and lower-case letters, numbers, and special characters. It is important that your password not be "guessable" and not contain words that can be found in the dictionary. For instance, names of your children or pets are not good password choices, nor is any variation of your address or phone number.

All that said, how does one come up with a password that will be safe from hacking, but easily remembered? Our suggestion is to think of a phrase that you are not likely to forget and generate a password using the first letters of the words in that phrase. For instance, the phrase "UNIX is a Four-Letter Word"[3] might yield the password "U!a4Lw". See the connection?

---

[1] The UNIX operating system is a product of AT&T and was developed in the early 1970's.

[2] Consult your local Yellow Pages for ISPs in your area.

[3] Christopher C. Taylor, "UNIX is a Four Letter Word . . . and Vi is a Two Letter Abbreviation".

Finally, as if enough has not been said about passwords, there are two more "shoulds" that need to be mentioned. First, it is not a good idea to use the same password for multiple accounts. In the rare event that your password is guessed on one machine, you do not want the culprit to gain access to your other accounts. Second, you should discipline yourself to change your password(s) periodically, and *always* change it if you suspect that it has been compromised in any way.

L A B   1 . 1

LOGGING IN USING FTP AND TELNET

There are two methods of accessing your shell account once it has been established and you have connected according to the instructions from your ISP.

FTP

As previously discussed, the File Transfer Protocol (FTP) is a method of copying files from one computer to another. There are a number of FTP programs available. Fetch is a popular shareware[4] program for the Macintosh. WS-FTP and CuteFtp are good choices for Windows and NT platforms. UNIX and DOS users are likely to find that FTP is available directly from the command line.

Regardless of the program you choose, there are a few basic things you need to know. First and foremost, you need to know your destination, or target, address. This can be a machine name, URL, and/or IP address, depending on how the destination machine is set up. You will also need to know your user ID and password at the destination, unless you are going to an anonymous FTP site[5].

Once you are connected, you are ready to copy files back and forth between your local machine and the remote machine. First, you will need to specify the type of file(s) you are transferring, indicating binary for images and compiled programs and ASCII for text files such as your HTML documents. Then, keeping in mind that the local machine (the computer running the FTP program) is the actor, you will use the following commands:

---

[4] All shareware and freeware programs mentioned in this document are currently available for download at www.tucows.com.

[5] While they are not as prolific as they used to be, anonymous FTP sites are a popular means of making documents and software available for download by the general public. More often than not, the login ID for any anonymous site will be the word "anonymous" and the password will be your valid electronic mail address.

get   Copy a file from the remote machine to the local machine.
Example: `get myfile.html`

mget   Copy multiple files from the remote machine to the local machine.
Example: `mget*.html`

(* is what is known as a wildcard, something that will be discussed in greater detail later on. In this case, we have asked FTP to transfer all files that end with the extension `.html`.)

put   Copy a file from the local machine to the remote machine.
Example: `put myfile.html`

mput   Copy multiple files from the local machine to the remote machine.
Example: `mput *.html`

How you issue these commands will differ depending on the program you are using. You should consult the documentation and help sections of the software for specifics. The following is an annotated sample session that illustrates using FTP in either DOS or UNIX.

A SAMPLE FTP SESSION

```
northshore% ftp webclass.merrimack.edu
Connected to webclass.merrimack.edu.
220-
220-          Eco Software, Inc. Unauthorized access is
prohibited.
220-
220 sparky4 FTP server (Version wu-2.4(1) Mon Jul 29
18:00:46 EDT 1996) ready.
```

Login.
```
Name (webclass.merrimack.edu:arlyn): webclass
331 Password required for webclass.
Password:
230 User webclass logged in.
```

Print working directory to see where we are.
```
ftp pwd
257 "/home/web/webclass.merrimack.edu" is current di-
rectory.
ftp cd virtual_html/ahubbell
250 CWD command successful.
```

List the directory.
```
ftp ls
200 PORT command successful.
150 Opening ASCII mode data connection for file list.
textcounter.tar
welcome.shtml
226 Transfer complete.
32 bytes received in 0.032 seconds (0.99 Kbytes/s)
```

Set transfer protocol to binary.
```
ftp bi
200 Type set to I.
```

Copy `textcounter.tar` from remote to local server.
```
ftp get textcounter.tar
200 PORT command successful.
150 Opening BINARY mode data connection for
textcounter.tar (30720 bytes).
226 Transfer complete.
local: textcounter.tar remote: textcounter.tar
30720 bytes received in 0.1 seconds (2.9e+02
Kbytes/s)
```

Set transfer protocol to ASCII.
```
ftp as
200 Type set to A.
```

Copy `welcome.shtml` from remote to local server.
```
ftp get welcome.shtml
200 PORT command successful.
150 Opening ASCII mode data connection for
welcome.shtml (174 bytes).
226 Transfer complete.
local: welcome.shtml remote: welcome.shtml
182 bytes received in 0.058 seconds (3.1 Kbytes/s)
```

Copy `test.html` from local to remote server.
```
ftp put test.html
200 PORT command successful.
150 Opening ASCII mode data connection for test.html.
226 Transfer complete.
local: test.html remote: test.html
1953 bytes sent in 0.019 seconds (1e+02 Kbytes/s)
200 PORT command successful.
150 Opening ASCII mode data connection for file list.
```

```
test.html
textcounter.tar
welcome.shtml
226 Transfer complete.
43 bytes received in 0.047 seconds (0.89 Kbytes/s)
```

Quit FTP session.
```
ftp quit
221 Goodbye.
northshore%
```

TELNET

Whereas FTP facilitates moving files back and forth between computers, telnet allows you to login directly to a remote machine and do your work there. Again, there are many programs available: CRT, for example, for Windows, and NCSA Telnet for the Mac. As with the various FTP clients, you will need to review the help documentation for your particular program regarding how to use it. A generic UNIX/DOS-style telnet session looks as follows:

```
shell3% telnet webclass.merrimack.edu
Trying 206.243.176.49 . . .
Connected to webclass.merrimack.edu.
Escape character is '^]'.

Shore.Net, a service of Eco Software, Inc. Access
restricted to Shore.Net hosting customers only.
Unauthorized access is prohibited.


SunOS UNIX (sparky4)

login: webclass
Password:
Last login: Wed Jun 30 21:09:34 from 216.20.65.70
                Welcome to the Shore.Net Virtual
Host server
                                    sparky4
        All use subject to terms and conditions of
membership agreement.
                Any access to other networks through
Shore.Net must
                comply with the rules appropriate for
that network.
```

If you do not agree with these rules, disconnect now.

For questions or assistance, mail support@shore.net or call (781) 593-3110.

Maintenance Windows and System Notes:

Window Type	Day	Time
Regular maintenance	Tues/Thur	0400 – 0600
Extended maintenance	Sun	0400 – 0800
Emergency	Any	0400 – 0600

see http://www.shore.net/services/policies for more information

o   The Membership Agreement is available at:
http://www.shore.net/services/policies/agreement.html
webclass.merrimack.edu%

LAB 1.1 EXERCISES

1.1.1   LOGGING IN USING FTP AND TELNET

a) What does FTP stand for?

_____

_____

b) When would you use FTP?

_____

_____

c) List the two transfer modes for FTP.

_____

_____

d) List the four major commands used to copy files and what they are used for.

_____

_____

e) What is telnet?

_____

_____

LAB 1.1 EXERCISE ANSWERS

1.1.1   ANSWERS

a)   What does FTP stand for?

Answer: File Transfer Protocol.

b)   When would you use FTP?

Answer: FTP is used to copy files from one machine to another.

c)   List the two transfer modes for FTP.

Answer: *bi*   –   *Binary*

           as   –   *ASCII*

d)   List the four major commands used to copy files and what they are used for.

Answer:

get   *Copies one file from the remote to the local machine.*

mget   *Copies multiple files from the remote to the local machine.*

put   *Copies one file from the local to the remote machine.*

mput   *Copies multiple files from the local to the remote machine.*

e)   What is telnet?

Answer: Telnet is an Internet protocol that allows the user to connect and login to a remote machine.

LAB 1.1 SELF-REVIEW QUESTIONS

1) Which of the following would qualify as a safe password?
   a) Hubbell
   b) 33StateStreet
   c) TaNSTa2F!
   d) All of the above
   e) None of the above

2) A password should not contain
   a) Special characters
   b) Upper- and lower-case letters
   c) English words
   d) Numbers

3) An example of an ASCII file is
   a) An image
   b) A compiled program
   c) An HTML document

4) Passwords should
   a) Never be changed
   b) Be changed periodically
   c) Be the same for all of your accounts

   Quiz answers appear in the Appendix, Section 1.1.

Regardless of the telnet method you use, once you have logged in, you are ready to start working in the UNIX environment. This brief tutorial is by no means meant to replace a full study of the UNIX operating system and its capabilities, but let's take a look at some of the basic commands you will be using.

L A B   1 . 2

BASIC UNIX COMMANDS

man   Displays UNIX manual pages.

man is the UNIX equivalent of "help," and will display detailed information about any given command that has a man page (see Figure 1.1).

EXAMPLE:

Shell3% man whoami

pwd   Displays (prints) the working directory.

This command answers the question, "Where am I?" with a directory path. This information will become more important to you as you start setting up multiple directories in your Web site. A common problem is losing track of where you are during a telnet session; pwd gives you the answer.

EXAMPLE:

shell3% pwd
/home/2/a/arlyn
shell3%

ls   Lists the current directory.

The ls command by itself displays all of the user file and directory names in your current directory.

Note that directory names are followed by a '/'.

ls -alg   Lists the current directory with details.

ls -alg displays the contents of your current directory, including system (dot) files that con-

Figure 1.1 ■ The UNIX man page for whoami.

tain instructions for your account (you might want to leave these alone for the time being), as well as access permissions, owners, file sizes, and date and time last modified. See Figure 1.2 for an example.

whoami   Who am I?

This command displays your user ID.

EXAMPLE:

```
shell3% whoami
arlyn
```

```
shell3 - SecureCRT                                    _ □ ×
File  Edit  View  Options  Transfer  Script  Window  Help

shell3% ls -alg
total 1979
drwx--x--x  10 arlyn     web         2560 Jul 10 17:41 ./
drwxr-xr-x 385 root      users       6656 Jul 10 00:08 ../
-rw-------   1 arlyn     web         1926 Nov  6  1998 .Xauthority
drwx------   2 arlyn     web          512 Apr 14 11:32 .elm/
-rw-------   1 arlyn     web       447657 Jul 10 17:31 .mail
-rw-------   1 arlyn     users        235 Jul  9 16:57 .newsrc
-rw-------   1 arlyn     users        235 Jul  9 16:51 .oldnewsrc
-rw-r--r--   1 arlyn     web          144 Oct 14  1997 .profile
-rw-------   1 arlyn     web           25 Jul  9 16:57 .rnlast
-rw-------   1 arlyn     web           18 Mar 19 13:15 .rnsoft
-rw-------   1 arlyn     users        176 Apr 22 12:05 .sig
drwxr-xr-x   2 arlyn     web          512 Oct 26  1998 .ssh/
drwx------   2 arlyn     web          512 Jul  8 09:30 Mail/
drwx------   2 arlyn     web          512 Nov  7  1998 News/
drwxr-xr-x   2 arlyn     web          512 Nov 16  1998 bin/
drwxr-xr-x   3 arlyn     users        512 Apr  2 18:30 book_files/
-rw-------   1 arlyn     web         7108 Nov  6  1998 html.rant
-rw-------   1 arlyn     web       199182 May  3  1996 humour
-rw-------   1 arlyn     users       2345 Jul  8 09:38 jon
-rw-------   1 arlyn     users       8249 Apr 26 17:50 learned
-rw-rw-r--   1 arlyn     web         1797 Oct  5  1998 macsvsunix.txt
drwx------   2 arlyn     users        512 Jun  7 21:25 mail/
-rw-------   1 arlyn     users       1444 May 12 09:18 mail-mappings
-rw-------   1 arlyn     users       2573 Feb 17 10:30 note
-rw-rw-r--   1 arlyn     web         3218 Nov  5  1998 programming
drwxr-sr-x   9 arlyn     web         5120 Jul  2 10:08 public_html/
-rw-------   1 arlyn     users       2732 Jun  1 09:29 rumination
-rw-------   1 arlyn     users    1272053 Jun 11 11:45 scrt232.exe
-rwxr-xr-x   1 arlyn     users        438 Feb  7 17:16 unix.humour*
-rw-------   1 arlyn     users       2591 Dec 21  1998 yuletide
shell3%
shell3%

Ready                      Telnet    34, 9    34 Rows, 80 Cols  VT100
```

Figure 1.2 ■ The `ls -alg` command.

```
shell3%
```

quota -v   Displays the quota, which is the amount of space you have available to you on the server.

cd   Changes the directory.

cd allows the user to move among the directories to which they have access.

EXAMPLE:

```
shell3% cd book_files
shell3%
```

Note that the request to change to the directory `book_files` returns nothing but the UNIX prompt—in this case, `shell3%`. Many UNIX commands are of the attitude "No news is good news," and will not return a message unless an error has occurred. For example, if we try to move into a directory that does not exist as we've specified, we will receive the following:

```
shell3% cd nonexistent_directory
nonexistant_directory: No such file or
directory
shell3%
```

The variations of `cd` we will be using are all of the same attitude; they are only listed and defined herein. The output of each successful request will look exactly like the initial `cd` `book_files` shown above. If you are ever in doubt as to whether you are where you think you are, issue the `pwd` command.

cd   Changes to your home directory, where you were when you first logged in.

cd ..   Moves up one directory.

LAB 1.2 EXERCISES

1.2.1 BASIC UNIX COMMANDS

a) Write the command that will tell you where you are on a UNIX server.

_____

_____

b) What is the command that displays your user ID?

_____

_____

c) Write the command that will move you into a subdirectory named `images`.

_____

_____

d) Write the command that will move you up one directory level.

_____

_____

e) Write the command that will move you back to your login directory.

_____

_____

f) Obtain help for the `date` command.

_____

_____

LAB 1.2 EXERCISE ANSWERS

1.2.1   ANSWERS

a)   Write the command that will tell you where you are on a UNIX server.

Answer: `pwd`

b)   What is the command that displays your user ID?

Answer: `whoami`

c)   Write the command that will move you into a subdirectory named `images`.

Answer: `cd images`

d)   Write the command that will move you up one directory level.

Answer: `cd  ..`

e) Write the command that will move you back to your login directory.

Answer: `cd`

f) Obtain help for the `date` command.

Answer: `man date`

LAB 1.2 SELF-REVIEW QUESTIONS

1) When using the `ls -alg` command, directory names are followed by a
   a) *
   b) .
   c) /
   d) ..

2) The `ls` commands displays
   a) Filenames
   b) Directory names
   c) Both of the above

3) `ls -alg` displays
   a) File and directory names
   b) Access permissions
   c) File sizes
   d) All of the above

4) UNIX will most often confirm the successful completion of a command.
   a) True
   b) False

Quiz answers appear in the Appendix, Section 1.2.

L A B   1 . 3

FILE AND DIRECTORY MANAGEMENT

cp   Copies one file to another.

The copy command is used to copy one file to another and is another example of a UNIX command that does not display output unless there is a problem. It should also be noted that the command will not warn you if you are about to over-write an existing file. UNIX, for better or worse, depending on how you feel about operating systems questioning your every command, usually assumes that you know what you are doing and does what you ask.

EXAMPLE:

```
shell3% cp toucans.GIF toucans.gif
shell3%
```

Notice the filenames `toucans.GIF` and `toucans.gif`. `toucans.GIF` is the original file and `toucans.gif` is the new file being created. The name of the new file was chosen to illustrate the case-sensitive nature of UNIX. `toucans.GIF` and `toucans.gif` are indeed two unique files.

```
shell3% ls toucans.*
toucans.GIF   toucans.gif
shell3%
```

This is going to be important to remember when you begin naming and accessing the files and directories on your Web site. The same case sensitivity applies to UNIX commands as well. `CP` is not the same as `cp`, and in fact, will generate an error.

cp -r   Copies recursively.

This variation of cp is used to copy a directory and its contents to another directory. cp alone will return an error if used with directories:

```
shell3% cp book_files book_files_new
cp: book_files: is a directory
shell3%
```

On the other hand, cp -r successfully creates a new directory:

```
shell3% cp -r book_files book_files_new
shell3%
```

mkdir   Makes a directory.

mkdir is used to create directories and subdirectories within your account.

EXAMPLE:

```
shell3% mkdir images
shell3%
shell3% ls
images/   toucans.GIF   toucans.gif
shell3%
```

mv   Moves files and directories.

mv is used to move files and directories from one place to another, as well as for renaming. Going back to our example files, we can change the name of toucans.GIF to toucans.Gif in this way:

```
shell3% mv toucans.GIF toucans.Gif
shell3% ls toucans.*
toucans.Gif toucans.gif
shell3%
```

The ls command verifies that the name of the file has been changed.

Now, note what happens when we use mv to move toucans.Gif into the images directory:

```
shell3% mv toucans.Gif images
```

```
shell3% ls toucans.*
toucans.gif images/
shell3%
```

`toucans.Gif` no longer appears in our directory listing because the file has been relocated to `images`.

rm   Removes files.

`rm` removes, or deletes, files and should be used with care as it does so without confirming your request. In UNIX, a request to remove a file is completed immediately; the file is not "marked" for removal at a later time, and there is no "trashcan" or "recycle bin" from which you can retrieve the file. Done is done.

EXAMPLE:

```
shell3% rm toucans.gif
shell3% ls toucans.gif
/usr/ucb/ls: No match.
shell3%
```

Notice that UNIX did not question our intent, and the subsequent `ls` does indeed confirm that our `toucans.gif` file is gone. The more severe consequences of using `rm` carelessly can be illustrated by combining the command with wildcards:

```
shell3% ls toucans.*
toucans.GIF toucans.Gif  toucans.gif
shell3% rm toucans.*
shell3% ls toucans.*
/usr/ucb/ls: No match.
shell3%
```

All three files are removed with nary a peep out of UNIX.

rmdir   Removes a directory.

`rmdir` is used to remove an empty directory. If the target of the command contains files or subdirectories, UNIX will complain:

```
shell3% rmdir remove_me
```

```
rmdir: directory "remove_me": Directory not
empty
shell3% cd remove_me
shell3% ls
file1 file2   file3
shell3% rm *
shell3% cd ..
shell3% rmdir remove_me
shell3%
```

**LAB
1.3**

Once we cd into remove_me, rm the existing files, and cd back one level, rmdir honors our request.

If you have directories you wish to remove without first removing the files and subdirectories they contain, you may, but please do so with care. The command is rm -r, and for the above example, would have been issued as such:

```
shell3% rm -r remove_me
shell3%
```

pico   Opens a simple full-screen editor on most UNIX servers.

A new file is opened by issuing the command with no argument, e.g., pico (see Figure 1.3). An existing file can be

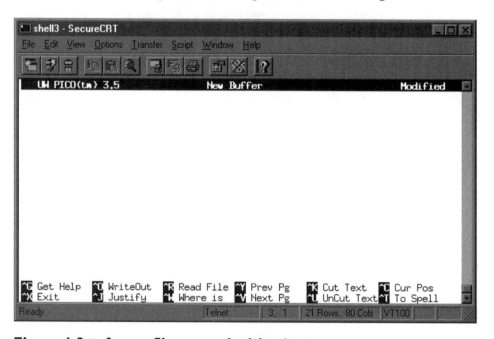

Figure 1.3 ■ A new file opened with pico.

opened by issuing the command followed by the name of the file you wish to modify, e.g., `pico myfile.html`. Your computer's arrow keys can be used to move among the text and control-character commands listed across the bottom of the editor window. The Help file, accessible via Control-G, details the editor's commands and their use.

Other text editors that are available on most UNIX servers are vi and Emacs. While it is entirely possible to create HTML files using an editor on a PC or Macintosh and then transfer to them to a UNIX server, it is strongly suggested that you become comfortable with the UNIX editor of your choice and work directly on the server. You will, in the long run, greatly appreciate bypassing the step of transferring a file every time it is changed.

LAB 1.3 EXERCISES

1.3.1 FILE AND DIRECTORY MANAGEMENT

a) What is the command to create a directory?

_____

_____

b) Copy a file named `Parrots` to another file named `Two_Parrots`.

_____

_____

c) Copy a directory named `Birds` to another directory named `Tweet`.

_____

_____

d) Rename the file `Parrots Two_Parrots.old`.

_____

_____

e) Copy `Two_Parrots.old` and `Two_Parrots` into the directory `Tweet`.

_____

_____

LAB 1.3 EXERCISE ANSWERS

1.3.1 ANSWERS

a) What is the command to create a directory?

Answer: `mkdir`

b) Copy a file named `Parrots` to another file named `Two_Parrots`.

Answer: `cp Parrots Two_Parrots`

c) Copy a directory named `Birds` to another directory named `Tweet`.

Answer: `cp -r Birds Tweet`

d) Rename the file `Parrots Two_Parrots.old`.

Answer: `mv Parrots Two_Parrots.old`

e) Copy `Two_Parrots.old` and `Two_Parrots` into the directory `Tweet`.

Answer: `cp Two.* Tweet`

LAB 1.3 SELF-REVIEW QUESTIONS

1) UNIX is case-sensitive.
   a) True
   b) False

2) `rmdir` will remove a directory and all of the files within it.
   a) True
   b) False

3) UNIX, by default, gives a warning if you are about to overwrite a file using `cp` or `mv`.
   a) True
   b) False

4) When `rm` is used with wildcards (*), UNIX will confirm the deletion of every file.
   a) True
   b) False

5) It is not possible to remove a directory unless the files it contains are removed first.
   a) True
   b) False

6) In UNIX, the commands `rm parrots` and `rm PARROTS` would remove the same file.
   a) True
   b) False

Quiz answers appear in the Appendix, Section 1.3.

LAB
1.3

L A B   1 . 4

FILE AND DIRECTORY PERMISSIONS

Perhaps one of the most important things to know in UNIX is how to grant and restrict access to your files and directories. For an HTML file to be readable over the Web, it must exist in a directory that is accessible to everyone and readable by everyone. The command used to change read, write, and execute permissions on files is chmod. Before looking at the command's syntax, however, let's take a quick look at a directory's and file's permissions as displayed with ls -alg.

The following two directory entries are for a directory named parrots and a file named pomegranate.html:

```
drwxr-xr-x  2 arlyn      users          512 Sep  2 22:08
parrots/
-rw-r--r--  1 arlyn      users          463 Jul 22 11:43
pomegranate.html
```

The permissions for the file and directory are shown in the first column and are broken down as follows:

Directory Flag	Owner Permissions	Group Permissions	World Permissions	
d	rwx	r-x	r-x	(parrots)
-	rw-	r--	r--	(pomegranate.html)

You'll note that the first column indicates whether the item is a file or a directory: d means it is a directory, - means it is a file. The remaining three columns detail the permissions for the owner of the file (u), the group that owns the file (g), and the rest of the world (o).

Value	Permission		Hexidecimal Value
r	Read		4
w	Write		2
x	Execute	(for a file)	1
	Enter	(for a directory)	

Based on the above, you can see that the directory `parrots` can be read by the owner, the group, and the world, only the owner can write to it, and everyone can enter it. The file `pomegranate.html` can be read by the world, but can be written to only by the owner.

Using `chmod`, one way to establish the permissions listed for the directory and file is as follows:

```
chmod 755 parrots
chmod 644 pomegranate.html
```

Take a minute to look at the `chmod` commands, the hex values of the permissions, and how they are grouped in the directory listings. In the case of the directory `parrots`, 755 is the result of adding together the numerical values for the owner permissions (rwx=4+2+1=7), the group permissions (rx=4+1=5), and the world permissions (rx=4+1=5). Using this logic, can you see the correlation between 644 and `rw-r--r--`for the file `pomegranate.html`?

Certainly, any number of permission variations can be established in this fashion, but 755 and 644 are the permission settings that are important for you to remember when making your HTML files available over the Web. 755 will allow browsers to enter and read or list directories, and 644 will allow them to read individual files. When creating new files and directories, always verify that the permissions are correct. While some servers will set them for you automatically, others will not, and this may lead to errors when a visitor tries to open your pages.

LAB 1.4 EXERCISES

1.4.1. FILE AND DIRECTORY PERMISSIONS

a) Based on the logic presented above, write the command to set the permissions for `pomegranate.html` such that only the owner of the file can read and write to it. The group and world will have no permissions at all.

_____

_____

b) Write the command to set permissions for `pomegranate .html` such that the owner, group, and world are only able to read the file.

_____

_____

c) Set the permissions for `parrots` such that only the owner can list and enter the directory.

_____

_____

d) Set the permissions for parrots such that the owner can list, write to, and enter the directory, and the group and world can only enter the directory.

_____

_____

LAB 1.4 EXERCISE ANSWERS

1.4.1 ANSWERS

a) Based on the logic presented above, write the command to set the permissions for `pomegranate.html` such that only the owner of the file can read and write to it. The group and world will have no permissions at all.

Answer: `chmod 600 pomegranate.html`

b) Write the comand to set permissions for `pomegranate.html` such that the owner, group, and world are only able to read the file.

Answer: `chmod 444 pomegranate.html`

c) Set the permissions for `parrots` such that only the owner can list and enter the directory.

Answer: `chmod 600 parrots`

d) Set the permissions for `parrots` such that the owner can list, write to, and enter the directory, and the group and world can only enter the directory.

Answer: `chmod 711 parrots`

LAB
1.4

LAB 1.4 SELF-REVIEW QUESTIONS

1) The numerical value of read+write+execute is
   a) 7
   b) 6
   c) 2

2) The numerical value of read+execute is
   a) 6
   b) 5
   c) 1

3) In most cases, files meant to be accessed by browsers over the Web must be readable by the
   a) Owner
   b) Group
   c) World

4) x means
   a) Executable
   b) Enter
   c) Both of the above

Quiz answers appear in the Appendix, Section 1.4.

C H A P T E R   1

TEST YOUR THINKING

The projects in this section use the skills you've acquired in this chapter. The answers to these projects are available to instructors only through a Prentice Hall sales representative and are intended to be used in classroom discussion and assessment.

The only way to get comfortable with the UNIX operating system is to use it. As suggested, you should obtain a UNIX shell account and start working with the commands discussed in this chapter. Find out from your provider the specifics of setting up a Web site on their server. Practice creating directories and files, setting appropriate permissions, and transferring files back and forth between the server and your local computer.

1) Create a couple of directories in the web area of your account: Images and Content. Make sure the permissions are set so that you will be able to create and modify files within them, and others will be able to browse the files from the web.

2) Using the ftp program of your choice, transfer a few files from your local machine to the directories you created. Put graphics in your Images directory and plain text in Content.

3) Double-check the transferred files for proper permissions. Reset them if necessary.

CHAPTER 2

SOME THOUGHTS ON SITE DEVELOPMENT AND MAINTENANCE

Tomorrow night I appear for the first time before a Boston audience—4000 critics.

Samuel Langhorne Clemens
Letter to Pamela Clemens Moffet (November 9, 1869)

A bad beginning makes a bad ending.

Euripides
Aeolus, Frag. 32

CHAPTER OBJECTIVES

In this chapter, you will learn about:

Unless you are creating a Web site simply as an exercise or for your own personal enjoyment, it is important to keep in mind that every person that visits your pages is a critic. And, unlike Mr. Clemens facing a Boston audience of 4000 critics, you are facing the Internet with millions of critics. Hence, it is wise to think a Web site through on many different levels prior to writing code for the pages.

CHAPTER EXERCISE

Write a short description of a Web site you would like to create. In a few short paragraphs, state the overall purpose of the site and detail what sort of information you would like to include.

_____

_____

_____

_____

_____

_____

_____

_____

_____

_____

_____

_____

_____

_____

_____

L A B   2 . 1

TECHNICAL
CONSIDERATIONS

As the technical capabilities of Web pages increase by the month, it is easy to forget that, more often than not, the technical capabilities of the audience at large do not. Whether by choice or necessity, not everyone in the world has access to the fastest connections, the best computers, or the latest browsers. It is critical to take these factors into account early in the development of any Web site and decide how these varying factors are (or are not) going to be addressed. If done intelligently and with care, it is perfectly valid to opt to cater to a specific technical subset of the general population, but to do so unwittingly is not.

BROWSERS

Netscape and Microsoft Internet Explorer are the most popular browsers at this writing, and the more recent versions are capable of rendering almost anything a Web developer might throw at them. Still, it is important to remember that these are not the only browsers people use, people do not always have the latest version, and some versions are not able to handle the features of the latest HTML standard. Additionally, there are other browsers in the field that have their own followings. Opera and Lynx are examples.

You should also think in terms of developing your pages so that they make sense to those using Web browsers that are enhanced for the visually impaired. Think about how your pages will work when they are read aloud by a blind person's browser—will they still get your message across to the visitor?

CONNECTIVITY

The speed of your typical visitor's Internet connection is going to be an important factor in the design of your site. While broadband services and dedicated lines are coming down in price and becoming more prevalent, it is still a fact that the majority of the online population is browsing the

Web over 28.8K and 33.6K dial-up connections. Because of slow download time, heavy use of graphics, animation, sound, and video often does not work well much of the time, and in the long run, may serve only to irritate those who visit your site.

Even if you do have access to state-of-the-art connectivity, think about what your audience on the whole will be using. By all means, if your site is geared toward and meant to be accessed by the technically privileged, go for the high-end elements of design and be liberal with your graphics and technical goodies. On the other hand, if you are catering to the at-home user, you may wish to either scale back a bit or offer an alternative set of pages to ensure your site's accessibility.

PERSONAL COMPUTERS

Just as you need to gear your site to the median connection capabilities of your visitors, you will also need to think about and design for the computers you expect your audience to have. Graphics and colors tend to be rendered differently on various machines, and what might be gorgeous on a PC screen, may be less than attractive on a Macintosh or UNIX monitor. When laying out your Web pages check your work on as many platforms as you can. Ideally, you should be able to adjust your design to accommodate everyone, but you may need to compromise in some cases.

L A B   2 . 2

CONSIDERING THE DEMOGRAPHICS OF YOUR AUDIENCE

When first thinking about the content and design of a Web site, one of the first questions you should ask yourself is, "Who do I want to visit this site?" Initially it may seem to be a trivial question, but coming up with a well-thought-out answer will go a long way toward the production of a successful Web site.

It helps to break the "Who" question down into a number of more specific questions, some of which might be:

- How old is my audience?
- Will my audience be predominantly male or female, or a mix?
- What are the interests of the people I want to visit my site?
- What is the income bracket of my expected audience?
- Where do the people in my audience live?
- How much education has the average visitor to my site completed?

The answers to these questions are going to dictate the appearance of your site, as well as the content. Sites geared toward younger audiences are often flashier when it comes to the use of color and graphics, while older visitors are likely to prefer a more subdued presentation. It would also seem that younger people are more apt to absorb information from a "busy" Web page than are older people. Animation, multiple frames, and sound are viable options for young audiences, but these elements may need to be toned down for older generations.

The language you use in your site will also be a result of answering these questions. Not only will you determine whether it is necessary to offer your text in several different languages, but also how formal the language used should be. Will your subject matter and expected audience support the use of slang and the latest lingo, or should you take pains to see that your prose is linguistically pure?

LAB
2.2

LAB 2.2 EXERCISE

2.2.1   CONSIDERING THE DEMOGRAPHICS OF YOUR AUDIENCE

Return to the description you wrote at the beginning of this Chapter and answer the demographics questions listed above. Determine the target audience of your Web site.

LAB 2.2 SELF-REVIEW QUESTIONS

1) It is safe to assume that a Web site will perform the same way on all platforms and with all browsers.
   a) True
   b) False

2) The majority of the Internet population browses Web sites using
   a) Dedicated lines
   b) Broadband, or cable connections
   c) 28.8K and 33.6K dial-up connections

3) Analyzing audience demographics helps determine
   a) General characteristics of desired Web site visitors
   b) Overall appearance of a Web site
   c) Style and formality of language
   d) All of the above

   Quiz answers appear in the Appendix, Section 2.2.

L A B   2 . 3

THE IMPORTANCE OF CONTENT

In the midst of all the elements of Web site design and maintenance, the most important factor is your **content**. Content is what is going to draw people to your site and keep them coming back regularly.

Points to consider when developing the content of your site include, but are not limited to:

- **Relevance**—Are your prose and graphics relevant to the subject at hand? Does the information you present stay on topic or does it wander in many directions? Will a visitor look at a graphic on one of your pages and ask, "Why on earth did they put that there?" As with any body of work meant for publication, your Web site's content must be engaging, cohesive, and it must stick to the point.

- **Accuracy**—It is critical that the information you provide be accurate. Be absolutely certain, to the best of your capabilities, that the facts, dates, and quotes you publish are correct. Opinions should be clearly stated as such and should not be left to be construed as fact.

- **Timeliness**—Be careful when publishing dated material or announcing future events. Announcements regarding future events should be either removed once the date has passed or turned into reports of the events as they occurred. Calendars should be maintained so that your visitor is not left looking at schedules that are months or even years out-of-date. Information that is no longer true or has changed in any way must be updated.

- **Spelling and grammar**—Proofread your documents as though they were chapters of a doctoral thesis. While slang and informal language may be acceptable under various circumstances, typos, spelling errors, and bad grammar are not. In the end, no matter how good your content might be, you will lose credibility in very short order if you allow errors such as these into your pages.

- **Originality**—Develop the content of your Web site with an eye toward creating something new. Ask yourself repeatedly, "Have I seen this before?" What are you offering to the public that they cannot get anywhere else, be it a new product, original art or literature, or simply a new and better way of presenting information?

- **Give something away**—The idea of getting something for nothing is always a draw and people will visit your site time and again if you offer them something free of charge. Tips of the week, recipes of the month, interviews, book reviews, and screensavers made available for download, changed regularly, are popular examples of this sort of content.

LAB
2.3

L A B   2 . 4

WEB SITE LAYOUT

How your visitors navigate through your Web site is critical and should not be left to chance. Presumably you will have a number of pages and, while you cannot completely dictate how people move among them, you can control their progress to a certain extent.

To this end, it is useful to produce a site map for your project. A site map is nothing more than a diagram of your Web site, a flowchart illustrating the pages you wish to include and how you intend to link them together. Taking the time to lay out your site graphically, either on paper with a pencil and a template or on a computer with appropriate software, allows you to think about its structure alone, and will ensure that your pages are connected in a logical fashion. Your map will also very quickly start to illustrate the depth, or number of levels, involved in your site.

**LAB
2.4**

Consider Figure 2.1, which shows a map for a fictitious school's Web site.

At this point, there are five pages planned for this site: My School (the "home page"), Courses, Faculty, Calendar, and Syllabi. The lines connect-

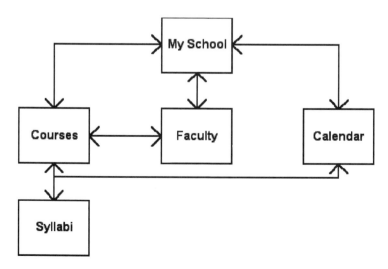

Figure 2.1 ■ A simple site map.

ing the rectangles represent links between the various pages. While some authors prefer to use the tactic of linking every page to every other page, particularly on small sites, this is not always the best way to do things. It is necessary to think about how the information on the pages fits together and what your visitor might want to see next.

In this example, a few decisions were made regarding links. First, only the first level of pages link directly back to the home page. Syllabi, while it can be argued that a link home might be useful there, only links back to Courses. From the Courses page, one can go to Faculty, Calendar, or Syllabi. The reasoning here is that as an individual reads the course descriptions, they may immediately wish to access details associated with a particular class: a professor's biography, a course syllabus, or dates when the class might be offered. The Calendar page is not linked to either Faculty or Syllabi, reflecting the opinion that a visitor will probably not want or need to make those connections directly.

Link logic, to a certain extent, is clearly a matter of opinion. It is up to you, the site designer, to determine how best to set up your links. Too few will prevent the visitor from finding everything you have to offer on your site, and too many will result in your visitor not knowing where to go next.

LAB 2.4 EXERCISE

2.4.1   WEB SITE LAYOUT

Create a small site map for your intended Web site. Decide what your first five or six pages will be about and illustrate how you plan to link them together.

LAB 2.4 SELF-REVIEW QUESTIONS

1) Every page on a Web site must link to every other page.
   a) True
   b) False

2) When developing a Web site, one should include as many links to as many similar sites as possible.
   a) True
   b) False

3) A Web designer can, to some extent, control how a visitor moves through a site's pages.

    a) True

    b) False

Quiz answers appear in the Appendix, Section 2.4.

<u>L A B   2 . 5</u>

WEB PAGE LAYOUT

You will find it helpful to set a standard page layout for your site early on, and once again, you will want to document the layout in a way that you will be able to reference later on. A sample page layout, the home page for the school site illustrated in Figure 2.1, can be seen in Figure 2.2.

As you can see, the top of the page is reserved for a banner graphic and the page title, a column of links will appear below them and to the left, and the balance of the page will be filled with content. It is a good idea to remember that, at least in the western world, a person's eye tends to move from top to bottom and left to right when looking at a page of printed material. For this reason, the top left block of a page is its most valuable real estate, as it is where the eye lands first by default. This is where you will place the items that you want to be noticed first. You may wish to take your page layout even further and block out your content areas, illustrating the positioning of text and graphics.

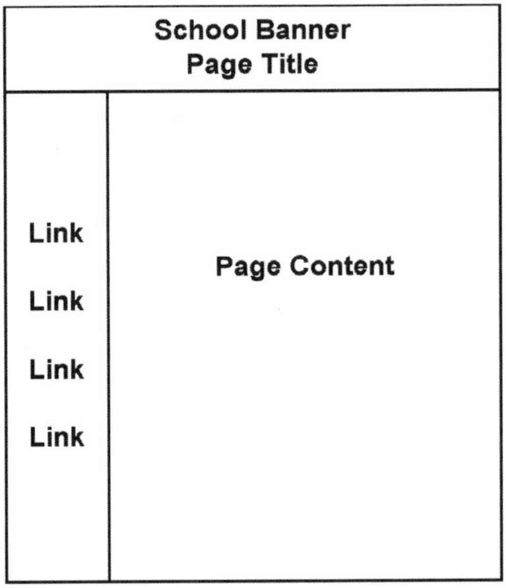

Figure 2.2 ■ A simple page layout.

Setting a page layout in no way means that every single page on your site must be exactly the same. It is, however, a good idea to maintain a certain degree of uniformity so that visitors know where they are and are not constantly being distracted from your content by new layouts. Very often, as the information on pages becomes more and more specific, the tendency is for the pages themselves to become plainer and plainer. For instance, on our school site, if papers written by faculty members were linked to the faculty page, it might make sense to leave out the school banner and page title and only include text links to appropriate pages at the top and bottom of each paper.

Laying out individual pages prior to writing any code also provides a graphical sanity check with regard to how much you are trying to include on a single page. If the layout starts to look busy, you know the Web page itself will be even worse and it is time to rethink the primary purpose of the page.

LAB 2.5 EXERCISE

2.5.1 WEB PAGE LAYOUT

Think about what you want to include on the home page of your Web site and produce a graphical page layout for that page. Develop another layout for your secondary pages.

LAB 2.5 SELF-REVIEW QUESTIONS

1) Only one page layout may be used for a Web site.
   a) True
   b) False

2) In the western world, the most valuable position on a Web page is the
   a) Top center
   b) Center of the page
   c) Top left

3) Setting page layout early on helps to
   a) establish page uniformity
   b) arrange page content
   c) decide the amount of content to be included
   d) all of the above

   Quiz answers appear in the Appendix, Section 2.5.

LAB 2.6

THE IMPORTANCE OF REGULAR MAINTENANCE

As we learned earlier, it is extremely important that the content of your Web site remain timely. This requires regular maintenance, a task that should be addressed early on, including how often the site will be updated and who is going to do it.

Site maintenance should also include routine reviews of all links, particularly those to addresses outside your site. The links themselves should be tested with a browser to confirm that they still work, and the content of the target site should be scanned to make sure that the material is still what you expect it to be. Web sites move and change, sometimes requiring you to change a link address or even remove it entirely.

Any time system changes occur on your Web server, it is well-advised that your Web site be thoroughly reviewed. Operating system upgrades and changes may have devastating effects on how your site behaves, in the worst case leaving it completely broken. Ask your system administrator to keep you informed of changes that may affect you and find out what you need to do to keep your site functioning properly.

Finally, as Web presentation evolves, you will find that you will need to periodically overhaul your site to keep up with current trends. Outdated Web sites quickly become unattractive and cumbersome when compared to others that have been revamped to embrace the newer standards. You will do well to remember that a Web site is the epitome of a living document in style as well as content.

**LAB
2.6**

CHAPTER 2

TEST YOUR THINKING

The projects in this section use the skills you've acquired in this chapter. The answers to these projects are available to instructors only through a Prentice Hall sales representative and are intended to be used in classroom discussion and assessment.

Brainstorm for an idea for a second Web site to work on and repeat the exercises you completed while working through this chapter.

1) Write a brief description of the site, stating its purpose and what should be included as content.

2) Determine the demographics of your audience and think about how the characteristics of your expected visitors will affect the style of this new site.

3) Develop a site map, illustrating the first few levels of pages and how they will be linked together.

4) Create page layouts for the home and secondary pages.

CHAPTER 3

HTML I

In creating, the only hard thing's to begin. . . .

James Russell Lowell
A Fable for Critics (1848)

L A B   3 . 1

WHAT IS HTML?

HTML, Hypertext Markup Language, is a system of elements that was originally meant to *suggest* how a document should be presented over the Web. Its primary purpose, when it was first introduced in the early 1990's, was to convey information that would be readable over the Web by users on many different platforms[1]. The first versions of the language allowed for only the simplest formatting of documents.

HTML has evolved over time, allowing Web page authors to be more and more specific with document formatting and appearance. New elements have emerged as well as whole new methods for displaying information. Some have been embraced as standards, some have been scorned and labeled as the beginning of the end of HTML and the Web (remember the infamous `<BLINK>` element), and some caused utter consternation among authors and browsers alike in that they were not universally understandable by all the browsers. The latest example of this is Cascading Style Sheets, which, while not exactly HTML, are yet to be interpreted in a uniform fashion by all browsers. "Browser wars" have developed and HTML users, both authors and Web page visitors, have divided into distinct camps with regards to the evolution of the language.

HTML is a series of elements and attributes that are used to suggest effects and where those effects should begin and end. As an example, take a look at the following sentence:

> I want the word **cat** to be bold.

The bolding of the word **cat** was achieved here by clicking the Bold button of the word processor before typing the word and clicking it again at the end. HTML works in a similar way and the code for the sentence is:

```
I want the word <B>cat</B> to be bold.
```

It really is frighteningly simple. The trick is to keep track of your beginning and ending elements as your documents become more complicated.

---

[1] More information about the development and evolution of HTML can be found at http://www.w3.org/MarkUp/MarkUp.html.

LAB 3.1 EXERCISES

3.1.1 WHAT IS HTML?

Write the HTML code needed to produce the following three sentences:

a) I want the word cat to be bold.

_____

_____

b) I want the word **cat** to be **bold**.

_____

_____

c) I want the word cat to be bold.

_____

_____

LAB 3.1 ANSWERS

3.1.1 ANSWERS

a) **I want the word cat to be bold.**

   Answer: `<BOLD>I want the word cat to be bold.</BOLD>`

b) I want the word **cat** to be **bold**.

   Answer: `I want the word <BOLD>cat</BOLD> to be <BOLD>bold</BOLD>.`

c) **I** want the word cat to be bold.

   Answer: `<BOLD>I</BOLD> want the word cat to be bold.`

LAB 3.1 SELF-REVIEW QUESTIONS

1) HTML is
   a) A programming language
   b) A means of suggesting document presentation

2) All HTML elements are understood by all Web browsers.
   a) True
   b) False

   Quiz answers appear in the Appendix, Section 3.1.

L A B   3 . 2

TEXT EDITORS VS. HTML EDITORS AND PUBLISHERS

There are many who would argue against the necessity of learning HTML, what with all of the WYSIWYG (What You See is What You Get) HTML software and publishers available on the market today. Programs such as Microsoft FrontPage and Adobe PageMill, as well as smaller programs like HotDog, allow the Web page author to create effects by highlighting text and clicking a button. What could possibly be wrong with that? Why bother with learning the actual elements and operating systems that support the Web? Why is it so strongly suggested here that you use a text editor to create your first Web pages, if not all of them in the future?

The main point is that HTML is a *language,* and that as with any language, it is essential to learn the basics if one is going to create elegant and useful output. An analogy might be that one cannot expect to build a car without understanding all of its parts. While the individual may be able to drive the car and perform routine maintenance such as changing the oil and filling it with gas, they will never be able to create a bigger and better car from scratch. Likewise with HTML, a thorough understanding of the language and the ability to work with it in its raw form will allow you to be more creative and efficient in the future.

Typing in your HTML with a text editor, while tedious after the newness of the subject has worn off, allows you to learn the intricacies and syntax of the language as you go along. You will also be able to maintain a level of control over your documents that is not easily achieved when using HTML editors and publishers. Many editors and publishers will dictate how your pages appear, depending on your choice of templates, as well as force specific site structures that they understand. These programs also have a tendency to add a great deal of extraneous code that often makes source documents difficult to read and modify in the future.

This is not to say HTML editors and publishers are all bad and should not be used at all. Once you have gained a thorough understanding of the language and how to structure a Web site, the programs can be useful tools. Various publisher features, in fact, are valuable to the author who is responsible for large sites. Link validation and the ability to load entire sites to a server with a single command are two features that are highly favored by professional Web site designers. Some publishers also have the ability to probe an existing Web site and produce a site map, including link logic—something that can be invaluable to an individual taking over an existing site.

In the end, it is your choice. It is, however, a fairly global opinion that the text editors should be used for learning and development and that the editing and publishing tools are excellent for maintenance.

L A B   3 . 3

BROWSER CONSIDERATIONS

In the past, Web browsers presented a much greater headache to Web designers than they do now. Yet, different browsers will still render your HTML in slightly different ways, different enough so that it is important to keep them in mind. Most designers keep a number of browsers on hand for reviewing pages in development. Particularly when using more advanced elements, such as those dealing with tables and frames, you may find that one browser's rendering of your code may not be the same as that of another. You may also find that some browsers are more forgiving than others when dealing with errors in HTML code. While one may be able to display a page containing errors, another may stumble and fail to display the page at all.

A dramatic example of rendering differences can be found in the comparison of Figures 3.4 and 3.5 later in this chapter. Figure 3.4, Netscape, displays a very simple page, including a header and an image in a way that most of us are used to seeing them. Figure 3.5 is what Lynx, a text-only browser, produces from the same code. You will note that the header is placed differently on the page and the image has been replaced by less than meaningful text. In this case, the content as well as the format of the page have changed. The image, which is presumably the cat called Fitch, is gone, and the individual viewing the page is left to wonder what exactly [INLINE] might be (the ALT attribute remedies this somewhat and will be discussed later on).

Lest you think that Lynx is the only browser to handle images this way, keep in mind that there are people who turn off image loading on their graphical browsers. This may be done to increase the speed of page downloads, decrease clutter on a page, or for any number of other reasons, but the result is the same. The appearance of your page will be changed and therefore may not be as attractive or useful as you might have originally thought.

All this said, it is impossible to ensure that your pages will be displayed exactly the same way by all browsers. It is, however, a worthwhile effort to review your work with as many browsers as possible and to be aware of their limitations.

LAB
3.3

LAB 3.4

HTML DOCUMENT STYLE

Pay attention to your document style when writing HTML code. Your style, or how you lay out and comment your code, should make your HTML easy to read and understand for both you and others who may have to edit it in the future. Use of comments and white space are essential to this end. Deciding early on whether to code your elements in upper- or lower-case, how to name your files (remembering that UNIX is case-sensitive!), and how to use indentation will make your life easier when you have to return to your HTML files for additional work.

On the other hand, the browser interpreting your HTML code will pay no attention at all to your HTML style. You will find that, in most cases, browsers will treat any amount of white space—a return, a tab, or multiple spaces—as a single space. An illustration of this fact can be seen in a quick analysis of Figures 3.1 – 3.5.

Figure 3.1 is a very simple HTML document which, when read with a browser, displays the page found in Figure 3.4 and Figure 3.5. The file has been written so that it is easy to read and edit. Figure 3.2 is the exact same text minus the carriage returns and additional white space that make it so easy to read. In Figure 3.3, we changed the line "I have a cat named Fitch" such that the individual words are separated by tabs and carriage returns. As different as the documents in Figures 3.2 and 3.3 look from that shown in Figure 3.1, they are displayed in exactly the same way. The actual Web page generated by all three documents is represented by Figure 3.4 and Figure 3.5.

Figure 3.1 ■ The original HTML document.

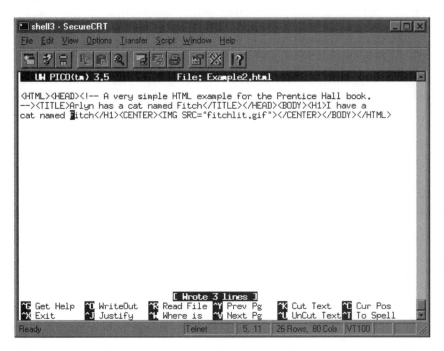

Figure 3.2 ■ Document text minus carriage returns and white space.

```
<HTML>
<HEAD>
<!-- A very simple HTML example for the Prentice Hall book. -->
<TITLE>Arlyn has a cat named Fitch</TITLE>
</HEAD>

<BODY>
<H1>I
        have a cat
                    named



Fitch</H1>

<CENTER>
<IMG SRC="fitchlit.gif">
</CENTER>

</BODY>
</HTML>
```

Figure 3.3 ■ Document text including tabs and carriage returns.

I have a cat named Fitch

Figure 3.4 ■ The Web page as rendered by Netscape.

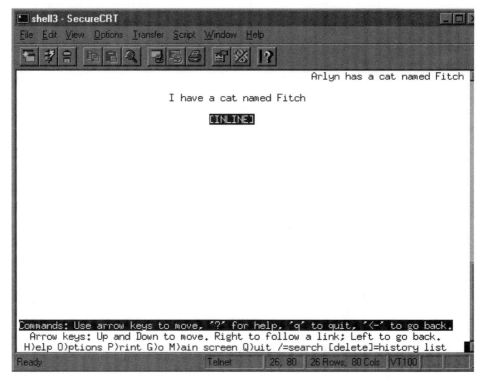

Figure 3.5 ■ **The Web page as rendered by Lynx.**

L A B 3 . 5

BASIC HTML ELEMENTS

Now that we have reviewed the concepts of authoring Web pages with regard to syntax and style, we can begin to look at the HTML elements themselves. To start, let's look at a stripped-down version of the HTML document shown in Figure 3.1 and review the elements in the order in which they appear. While the document was simple enough to start with, it is even easier to see the HTML elements and how they work with the content removed as it is in Figure 3.6.

\<HTML> \<HTML> indicates the beginning of an HTML document. While current browsers do not need this element to interpret a page properly, it is still good form to use it at the start of your documents.

**LAB
3.5**

Figure 3.6 ■ HTML elements only.

\<HEAD>	The \<HEAD> element is used to start the head of an HTML document, which is information that is read and processed but not displayed as part of the page body by a browser.
\<!—	\<!-- begins a comment, a general notation about the document which is included for future reference. Notes might include modification dates and who made the modifications, sources of information contained in the page, who the page was written for, and ideas for future content, among other things. Comments may be put anywhere in an HTML document, not just in the head, and should be used liberally.
--\>	End of comment.
\<TITLE>	The title of a document contains text that will appear on the top bar of the browser. It is also the text that is saved when an individual bookmarks a page with a browser. For this reason, it is a good idea to make certain that your title text is a good description of the page. The title is always included within the head of an HTML document.
\</TITLE>	End of title.
\</HEAD>	End of head.
\<BODY>	The \<BODY> element signifies the beginning of the content to be displayed by the browser.
\<H1>	Header elements delineate various "levels" of a document. \<H1> is, unless otherwise specified using style sheets, the largest and heaviest; \<H6> is the smallest and lightest.
\</H1>	End of header section.
\<CENTER>	\<CENTER> tells the browser to begin centering all of the following content.
\<IMG SRC>	Image Source displays the image indicated. In Figure 3.4 \<IMG SRC="fitchlit.gif"> displays an image called fitchlit.gif.
\</CENTER>	End centering and return to the default of left alignment for page content.
\</BODY>	End of the document body.
\</HTML>	End of the HTML document.

With these explanations in mind, return now to Figures 3.1 and 3.4 and review how the elements and browser display are related.

LAB 3.5 EXERCISES

3.5.1   BASIC HTML ELEMENTS

Copy the text in Figure 3.1 into a file of your own, either in your ISP account or locally, and start making small changes to it while checking the effects of the changes with a browser. Keep in mind that the image will be broken unless you replace it with another that you already have.

a) Experiment with the various header levels, replacing occurrences of H1 with H2, H3, H4, H5, and H6.

b) Move the <CENTER> element so that it appears before the header and observe the effect.

c) Remove the <IMG SRC> line and replace it with a line of plain text. Note the format and placement of the text when the file is viewed with a browser.

LAB
3.5

LAB 3.5 SELF-REVIEW QUESTIONS

1)   The style, or layout, of your HTML source file is important to
   a)   The browser rendering the code
   b)   The human reading the code

2)   Which HTML element's content is used as a description in a visitor's bookmark?
   a)   <HEAD> ... </HEAD>
   b)   <TITLE> ... </TITLE>
   c)   <H1> ... </H1>

3) Comments may appear

    a) Only within the head of an HTML document

    b) Anywhere in an HTML document

Quiz answers appear in the Appendix, Section 3.5.

LAB
3.5

L A B   3 . 6

MORE BASIC HTML ELEMENTS

Now that we have looked at the basic layout of an HTML document and how the elements work, let's continue with a few more elements. Our first HTML file has been enhanced to include the elements we will discuss and is shown in Figure 3.7. Figure 3.8 is Netscape's rendering of the new code.

Figure 3.7 ■ More HTML elements.

Figure 3.8 ■ Figure 3.7 rendered by Netscape.

**LAB
3.6**

`<IMG SRC>`   Image Source (revisited)

While this element was addressed briefly in the previous section, it warrants a bit more discussion now and will be revisited again in Chapter 4.

You will notice that the `<IMG SRC>` in Figure 3.7 contains a bit more information than was found in the element in Figure 3.1. Two attributes have been included: ALT and BORDER.

ALT allows you to include alternate text that will be displayed when a browser is not able to render images. This is also the text that will appear when the mouse cursor is placed over the image in the newer browsers. The content, or value, of the attribute is limited to 1024 characters. The ALT attribute should be included with every image and should be descriptive, not unlike your title. In many cases, it will be all that some people see of your images. In the case of invisible images being used as placeholders or to force spacing, ALT=" " should be used so that no text will appear if the image cannot be displayed.

The BORDER attribute allows you to place a border around an image. The border's width is measured in pixels, in this case 14. BORDER="0" will remove an image border if so desired, and is sometimes done when an image is used as a hyperlink.

<P> Paragraph

<P> . . . </P> is used to enclose text to be rendered as a paragraph. Regardless of the format of the text in the HTML document, the browser will arrange it into a proper paragraph. Note that <P> does not indent the first line of a paragraph unless it is specified to do so via a style sheet.

**
** Break

 signals a line break to the browser. In this case, it has been used to separate links onto separate lines at the bottom of the page. Note that multiple <BR> elements will force multiple blank lines between items for most browsers; some browsers require some sort of content to render the effect properly. , the non-breaking space, will ensure that your line breaks are acknowledged.

<A> Anchor

The anchor element is most often used with the HREF (hypertext link) attribute and specifies the target, or address, for a link, or text that can be clicked to go elsewhere. Figure 3.7 shows three types of HREF values: http, ftp, and mailto.

- http is used when you wish to take your visitor to another Web page.
- ftp indicates that the address is an FTP site and will allow the visitor to download files from a remote machine.
- mailto will allow the visitor to send mail to the specified address using their default browser's email program.

LAB 3.6

LAB 3.6 EXERCISES

3.6.1 MORE BASIC HTML ELEMENTS

Return to the HTML document you created in the exercises of section 3.2, make the following changes, and review them in at least one browser:

a) Add a link to http://www.prenhall.com/.

b) Add a link that will allow people to send mail to you at your email address.

c) Add back an image to the page and generate meaningful alternate text for it.

d) Add a border to your image and experiment with varying widths.

LAB 3.6 SELF-REVIEW QUESTIONS

1) The paragraph element (`<P>`, `</P>`) will indent the first line of a paragraph by default.
   a) True
   b) False

LAB 3.6

2) Multiple blank lines can be achieved with more than one of which element?
   a) `<P>`
   b) `<BR>`

3) Match the following HREF attributes to their correct uses:
   a) `http`   _____ download a file from a remote machine
   b) `ftp`   _____ send mail using the visitor's default email program
   c) `mailto`   _____ take the visitor to another page

4) The ALT attribute for an image
   a) Contains text that browsers that do not render images will display
   b) Contains text that will be displayed when the mouse is placed over an image
   c) Both of the above

5) The character limit for the ALT attribute is
   a) 100
   b) 512
   c) 1024
   d) Unlimited

6) The ALT attribute is required.
   a) True
   b) False

Quiz answers appear in the Appendix, Section 3.6.

CHAPTER 3

TEST YOUR THINKING

The projects in this section use the skills you've acquired in this chapter. The answers to these projects are available to instructors only through a Prentice Hall sales representative and are intended to be used in classroom discussion and assessment.

Using all of what you have learned in this chapter and referring back to the site description and map you created in Chapter 2, construct three or four small Web pages using a text editor (preferably pico in your UNIX shell account).

1) Include at least one image and provide appropriate decriptive alternate text for visitors with text-only browsers.

2) A visitor should never have to use the browser's back button to return to the previous page. Include appropriate back links on all of your pages.

3) Provide your visitors with the ability to send you email from each page.

HTML II

Enough! or Too Much.

William Blake
The Marriage of Heaven and Hell (c. 1793)

Always keep in mind that as your HTML and Web pages become more complex, it is critical to know when to stop. You will learn about a number of ways to format and customize your Web pages in this chapter, but remember, "Just because you can, doesn't mean you should."

L A B   4 . 1

INLINE, BLOCK, AND INVISIBLE ELEMENTS

HTML elements fall into three major categories: inline, block, and invisible. Keeping the categories of elements clear in your mind will be helpful while working with your code, especially when you start combining them to produce certain effects. Table 4.1 lists the elements that we will discuss, along with each element's category.

An inline element is an element that produces an effect or serves a function, but does not force a new line when its content is rendered. Content will continue to fill the current line and wrap onto the next unless a <BR> or block element is encountered.

Block-level elements render content on a new line. Refer back to the HTML code in Figure 3.7 and note that while the anchor elements require breaks in order for them to include a line feed, headers and paragraphs do not. Headers and paragraphs are defined as block elements.

Elements that are not actually displayed by a browser are referred to as invisible elements. While the browser may indeed process the contents of an invisible element, nothing is rendered on the actual Web page.

Table 4.1 ■ HTML Elements and Their Categories

Element	Effect	Category
`<!--`	Comment	Invisible
`A`	Anchor Link	Inline
`DD`	Definition Description	Block
`DL`	Definition List	Block
`EM`	Emphasis	Inline
`H1 - H6`	Headers 1 – 6	Block
`HEAD`	Document Head	Invisible
`I`	Italic	Inline
`IMG`	Image	Inline
`LI`	List Item	Block
`OL`	Ordered List	Block
`P`	Paragraph	Block
`PRE`	Preformatted Text	Block
`STRONG`	Strong Text	Inline
`TITLE`	Title Text	Invisible
`UL`	Unordered List	Block

L A B   4 . 2

TEXT STYLE ELEMENTS

HTML comes with a variety of text elements that allow you to change the style and appearance of your text. Many of these have been deprecated, or scheduled to be removed from the HTML standard, with the introduction of style sheets, but it is still worth learning the elements and how they are used. The elements are divided into two categories: content-based and physical.

Content-based style elements are the lesser used of the two, but are actually preferred over physical elements as they are more in keeping with the original HTML standards. These elements cause the browser to format the enclosed text according to the context, or meaning of the material, requiring the HTML author to pay attention to the real intent of a given format. The difference in display is non-existent for most of the standard browsers (see Figure 4.1), but for those meant for the blind or handicapped, the results can be critical.

There is no specific format assigned to content-based elements, though the defaults for most browsers are fairly consistent. The only requirement in rendering text formatted with a content-based element is that it be **different** from normal text in a manner that matches the intent of the format.

Figure 4.1 ■ **Physical vs. content-based elements.**

Content-based elements include, but are not limited to:

CITE	Bibliographic citations, such as books
CODE	Computer program source code
EM	Emphasized text
STRONG	Strong text

By contrast, physical elements dictate the appearance of the text with no variation. Whereas some browsers might render <EM>, which defaults to an italic font in most browsers, in a different way, <I> (italic) will always be displayed as italic.

Physical styles include:

B	Bold
BIG	Increases the size of text
BLINK	Blinks text
I	Italic
PRE	Pre-formatted text
SMALL	Decreases the size of text
SUB	Subscript
SUP	Superscript
TT	Mono-spaced font

More than one style element may be used to modify a single block of text. Pay attention, however, to the order of your opening and closing elements. For instance,

Make these words <B><I>bold and italicized</I></B>.

is perfectly valid code. On the other hand,

Make these words <B><I>bold and italicized</B></I>.

may produce unexpected results when viewed with a browser.

LAB 4.2 EXERCISES

4.2.1   TEXT STYLE ELEMENTS

Generate HTML code to produce the following text effects:

a) This effect is ***big, bold, and italicized.***

_____

_____

b) This effect is ^{superscript}.

_____

_____

c) This effect is $_{subscript}$.

_____

_____

d) This effect is big, bigger, and biggest.

_____

_____

LAB 4.2 EXERCISE ANSWERS

4.2.1   ANSWERS

a)   This effect is ***big, bold, and italicized.***

Answer: This effect is `<BIG><B><I>big, bold, and italicized</I></B></BIG>`.

or

This effect is `<BIG><STRONG><EM>big, bold, and italicized</EM></STRONG> </BIG>`.

b) This effect is ^{superscript.}

Answer: `This effect is <SUP>superscript</SUP>.`

c) This effect is _{subscript.}

Answer: `This effect is <SUB>subscript</SUB>.`

d) This effect is big, **bigger**, and **biggest**.

Answer: `This   effect   is   <BIG>big,   <BIG>bigger,   and <BIG>biggest.</BIG></BIG></BIG>`

LAB 4.2 SELF-REVIEW QUESTIONS

1) An inline element
   a) Displays content on a new line
   b) Does not display content on a new line

2) A block-level element
   a) Displays content on a new line
   b) Does not display content on a new line

3) Identify the following elements as block-level, inline, or invisible:

	Block-level	Inline	Invisible
`<!--`	____	____	____
`A`	____	____	____
`DD`	____	____	____
`DL`	____	____	____
`EM`	____	____	____
`H1 - H6`	____	____	____
`HEAD`	____	____	____
`I`	____	____	____
`IMG`	____	____	____
`LI`	____	____	____
`OL`	____	____	____
`P`	____	____	____
`PRE`	____	____	____
`STRONG`	____	____	____
`TITLE`	____	____	____
`UL`	____	____	____

4) Content-based elements
   a) Dictate the appearance of enclosed text
   b) Indicate that text should be rendered differently from surrounding text

5) Physical elements

    a) Dictate the appearance of enclosed text

    b) Indicate that text should be rendered differently from surrounding text

6) Identify the following elements as either physical or content-based:

	Physical	Content-based
SMALL	____	____
CITE	____	____
TT	____	____
BLINK	____	____
BIG	____	____
I	____	____
EM	____	____
SUP	____	____
B	____	____
PRE	____	____
STRONG	____	____
CODE	____	____
SUB	____	____

Quiz answers appear in the Appendix, Section 4.2.

L A B   4 . 3

LINKS

Links were introduced in Chapter 3, where we looked at a number of different HREF values, including the http, ftp, and mailto protocols. In this section, we will look at links in more detail.

ABSOLUTE VS. RELATIVE URLS

The URL, or HREF value, of a link can be written in two ways: absolute or relative. An absolute URL is the full address of the page you wish to go to, including the protocol, host name, and directory and filenames. For instance, in Figure 2.7 you see the following link:

```
<A HREF="http://www.shore.net/~arlyn/siteindex.html"
Index</A>
```

The syntax of the link includes all of the information the browser needs to find the referenced page: protocol, host name, directory, and filename. No interpretation is needed.

Relative URLs indicate target link addresses **relative** to the current page; the browser fills in the rest of the address based on information it already has. The example above can be rewritten as a relative address in a couple of different ways based on the fact that Example4.html, the HTML file, lives in the subdirectory Book, and siteindex.html is located one directory above it.

```
<A HREF="../siteindex.html">Index</A>
```

The notation here is the same as you saw in Chapter 1, and it means exactly the same thing. Recall that .. means to move up one level in the directory structure. The browser, in this case, fills in the balance of the address information it needs based on the current page and proceeds to the correct URL when the link is clicked.

A second relative URL for the same address would be:

```
<A HREF="/siteindex.html">Index</A>
```

In this case, the relative address indicates a return to the top level of the site to find `siteindex.html`. Again, the browser recalls the host name from the current page. The benefit of using relative URLs is that relocating your directory structures will require minimal amounts of HTML code modification. Also, directories can be renamed on-the-fly, without worrying about broken links.

LINKING TO A POINT WITHIN A DOCUMENT

You link to specified areas within a document with just a little more code. This is done in two parts, one in the link code and the other in the HTML document being referenced.

Suppose, for example, that you wanted to link to a section in `siteindex.html` called "book", where there were links to material having to do with the writing of this book. The relative link itself would be written as follows:

```
<A HREF="../siteindex.html#book">The Book</A>
```

#book tells the browser to go to the section of `siteindex.html` labeled "`book`" and display the Web page starting there.

The corresponding code in `siteindex.html` is:

```
<A NAME="book">
<LI><A HREF="Book/">THE BOOK</A>
```

The value of the NAME attribute serves as a label for a section of the document. Keep in mind that, as with all things in UNIX, the label is case-sensitive. The case you use in the URL must match the NAME value or the label will not be found.

A FEW WORDS ABOUT USING LINKS

Regardless of whether your links are embedded in the paragraph text of your document or grouped together into lists, they should be used carefully. Think back to the content discussion in Chapter 2 and recall the points of relevance and originality. Links, especially embedded links, should be relevant to your subject and enhance the information you have already provided. It does not make sense, nor will it support your credibility, to allow links to go too far off the main topic.

Links within your document text, embedded links, should be used sparingly and only when they will truly augment your content. Too many links will not only make the text difficult to read, but the visitor's comprehension of your material will suffer care of the jumping back and forth between pages should he choose to follow the links. Even worse, you may lose the visitor entirely via a link to an outside site.

It is wise to be conservative with your link lists. Again, consider the relevance of the links themselves. The originality of your list should also be addressed. What is it about the list that makes it different from others that already exist? A nice touch is to annotate a list of links, offering short descriptions or reviews of sites you are recommending to your visitors. Huge link lists with no comments whatsoever can be both confusing and cumbersome. Providing notes about your links will alleviate this.

Finally, remember without fail that all links must be reviewed frequently. It only takes a couple of broken links to drive your visitors away from your site forever.

LAB 4.3
4.3

LAB 4.3 EXERCISES

4.3.1 LINKS

a) Rewrite the following absolute URL link:

```
<AHREF="http://www.shore.net/~arlyn/Book/Example4.
html>Example 4</A>
```

as relative URLs for the following scenarios:

1) The document containing the link is in the `Book` directory.

2) The document containing the link is in the top-level directory, `~arlyn`.

3) The document containing the link is in a subdirectory of `Book` called `chapter1`.

_____

_____

4) The document containing the link is in a subdirectory of `chapter1`.

_____

_____

b) Write the code required for the link and within the link's target HTML document to access the "`goelsewhere`" section of `Example4.html`.

_____

_____

LAB 4.3 EXERCISE ANSWERS

4.3.1 ANSWERS

a) Rewrite the following absolute URL link:

**`<AHREF="http://www.shore.net/~arlyn/Book/Example4.`
`html>Example 4</A>`**

as relative URLs for the following scenarios:

1) The document containing the link is in the Book directory.

Answer: `<A HREF="Example4.html">`....

2) The document containing the link is in the top-level directory, `~arlyn`.

Answer: `<A HREF="Book/Example4.html">`....

3) The document containing the link is in a subdirectory of `Book` called `chapter1`.

Answer: `<A HREF="../Example4.html">`....

or

```
<A HREF="/Book/Example4.html">....
```

4) The document containing the link is in a subdirectory of `chapter1`.

Answer: `<A HREF="../../Example4.html">....`

or

```
<A HREF="/Book/Example4.html">....
```

b) Write the code required for the link and within the link's target HTML document to access the "goelsewhere" section of `Example4.html`.

Answer: The link: `<A HREF="Example4.html#goelsewhere">....`

The target: `<A NAME="goelsewhere">`

LAB 4.3 SELF-REVIEW QUESTIONS

1) `<A HREF="http://www.prenhall.com">PrenHall</A>` is an example of
   a) An absolute link
   b) A relative link

2) `<A HREF="../sometext.html">Text</A>` is
   a) An absolute link
   b) A relative link

3) `<A HREF="index.html#section2">Section 2</A>` links to
   a) A file named `index.html#section2`
   b) An area in `index.html` named `section2`
   c) Nothing; it is not a valid link

4) The proper syntax for labeling a section of an HTML file "section2" for the link in Question 3 would be
   a) `<!- NAME="section2"->`
   b) `<NAME="section2">`
   c) `<A NAME="section2">`

5) Document text should contain
   a) No links at all
   b) A conservative number of links only to augment the text
   c) As many links as possible

6) Link lists should be
   a) All-inclusive and as large as possible
   b) Selective, relevant, and original
   c) Non-existent

Quiz answers appear in the Appendix, Section 4.3.

LISTS

Lists, while they are not as popular as they used to be, can be very useful. They are a simple, universally recognizable means of formatting text and an excellent vehicle for producing formal outlines. Three list styles are available in HTML.

UNORDERED LISTS

Unordered lists are lists in which the order of the items is not important. Examples might be grocery or to-do lists, assuming that you do not list grocery items in the order that you encounter them in the store or the to-do items do not need to be completed in any order.

Figure 4.2 is an unordered list as displayed by Netscape, and Figure 4.3 is the HTML code for the list. You will notice that there are two elements associated with the list itself: `<UL>` ... `</UL>` and `<LI>`. Note that `<LI>` does **not** require an end element. You should also note that two of the list items are coded with the attribute TYPE, another deprecated attribute that is intended to be handled with style sheets, which allows you to specify the type of bullet to precede the list item content. The browsers support three standard bullets (although there are ways to incorporate

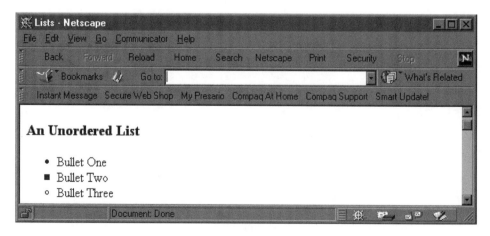

Figure 4.2 ■ An unordered list.

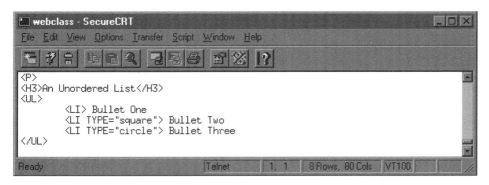

Figure 4.3 ■ The unordered list HTML.

your own custom bullets that will be discussed later): disc (the default), square, and circle.

**LAB
4.4**

ORDERED LISTS

As implied by their name, ordered lists are those in which items appear in a meaningful order. Notice that the HTML elements for an ordered list follow exactly the same logic as an unordered list. `<OL>` opens the list, `<LI>` signifies a list item, and `</OL>` closes the list (see Figures 4.4 and 4.5). Ordered lists rapidly become more interesting and sophisticated with the incorporation of the attributes `TYPE` and `START`.

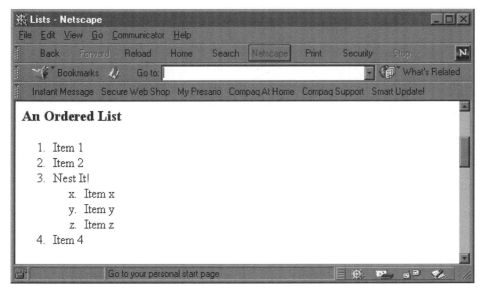

Figure 4.4 ■ An ordered list.

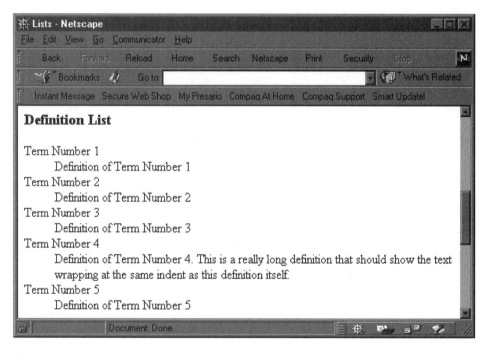

```
shell3 - SecureCRT
File  Edit  View  Options  Transfer  Script  Window  Help

<H3>An Ordered List</H3>
<OL>
        <LI> Item 1
        <LI> Item 2
        <LI> Nest It!
        <OL START="24" TYPE="a">
                <LI > Item x
                <LI> Item y
                <LI> Item z
        </OL>
        <LI> Item 4
</OL>

Ready                              Telnet    1, 1   13 Rows, 80 Cols  VT100
```

Figure 4.5 ■ The ordered list HTML.

```
Lists - Netscape
File  Edit  View  Go  Communicator  Help

  Back   Forward   Reload   Home   Search   Netscape   Print   Security   Stop      N

   Bookmarks      Go to:                                        What's Related

 Instant Message  Secure Web Shop  My Presario  Compaq At Home  Compaq Support  Smart Update!

Definition List

Term Number 1
      Definition of Term Number 1
Term Number 2
      Definition of Term Number 2
Term Number 3
      Definition of Term Number 3
Term Number 4
      Definition of Term Number 4. This is a really long definition that should show the text
      wrapping at the same indent as this definition itself.
Term Number 5
      Definition of Term Number 5

            Document: Done
```

Figure 4.6 ■ A definition list.

TYPE allows you to specify the type of numbering to use in any particular list. The recognized values are:

A   Upper-case letters

a   Lower-case letters

```
<H3>Definition List</H3>
<dl>
<dt>Term Number 1</dt>
<dd>Definition of Term Number 1</dd>
<dt>Term Number 2</dt>
<dd>Definition of Term Number 2</dd>
<dt>Term Number 3</dt>
<dd>Definition of Term Number 3</dd>
<dt>Term Number 4</dt>
<dd>Definition of Term Number 4. This is a really long definition
that should show the text wrapping at the same indent as this definition
itself.</dd>
<dt>Term Number 5</dt>
<dd>Definition of Term Number 5</dd>
</dl>
<BR><BR>
```

Figure 4.7 ■ The definition list HTML.

I	Upper-case Roman numerals
i	Lower-case Roman numerals
1	Arabic numerals

START tells the browser where to start the numbering for list items. The value of the START attribute is always numeric, even if the list type is alphabetic. Observe in Figures 4.4 and 4.5, START=24 starts the current list with the lower-case letter x.

DEFINITION LISTS

Definition lists are generally used to format terms and definitions (see Figure 4.6). While the elements used differ slightly from unordered and ordered lists, as can be seen in Figure 4.7, the idea remains the same. <DL> starts the list, <DT> ... </DT> encloses the term to be defined, and <DD> ... </DD> encloses the term's definition. </DL>, of course, ends the definition list.

LAB 4.4 EXERCISES

4.4.1 LISTS

a) Nesting lists, the practice of including lists within lists, is fairly common and a very simple example can be found in Figures 4.4 and 4.5. Nests also occur when the HTML author unwittingly leaves out end list elements. Finding such an error can result in a fair amount of frustration if the list is complicated and the code is not formatted so that the beginnings and ends of lists can be easily seen.

Reproduce the following set of nested lists and check your work with as many browsers as are available to you.

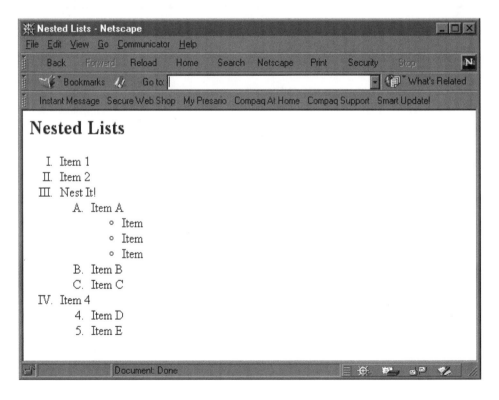

b) Earlier in this chapter, it was mentioned that there are ways to use your own graphics as bullets in an unordered list. One way is to vary the use of the definition list's code slightly so that a list might appear as it does here:

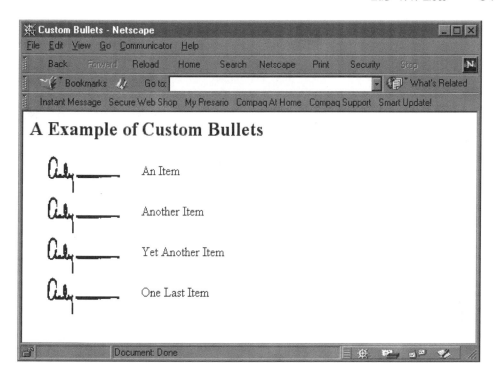

Review the definition list elements and reproduce this page.

LAB 4.4 EXERCISE ANSWERS

4.4.1 ANSWERS

a) Nesting lists, the practice of including lists within lists, is fairly common and a very simple example can be found in Figures 4.4 and 4.5. Nests also occur when the HTML author unwittingly leaves out end list elements. Finding such an error can result in a fair amount of frustration if the list is complicated and the code is not formatted so that the beginnings and ends of lists can be easily seen.

Reproduce the following set of nested lists and check your work with as many browsers as are available to you.

Answer:

LAB
4.4

```
shell3 - SecureCRT                                          _ □ ×
File  Edit  View  Options  Transfer  Script  Window  Help

<HTML>
<HEAD>
<TITLE>Nested Lists</TITLE>
</HEAD>
<BODY BGCOLOR="ffffff">
<H2>Nested Lists</H2>
<OL TYPE=I>
        <LI> Item 1
        <LI> Item 2
        <LI> Nest It!
        <OL TYPE=A>
                <LI > Item A
                        <UL>
                                <LI TYPE=CIRCLE> Item
                                <LI TYPE=CIRCLE> Item
                                <LI TYPE=CIRCLE> Item
                        </UL>
                <LI> Item B
                <LI> Item C
        </OL>
        <LI> Item 4
        <OL TYPE=A START=4>
                <LI> Item D
                <LI> Item E
        </OL>
</OL>
</BODY>
</HTML>

Ready                          Telnet      23  8   30 Rows, 80 Cols  VT100
```

b) Earlier in this chapter, it was mentioned that there are ways to use your own graphics as bullets in an unordered list. One way is to vary the use of the definition list's code slightly so that a list might appear as it does here:

Answer:

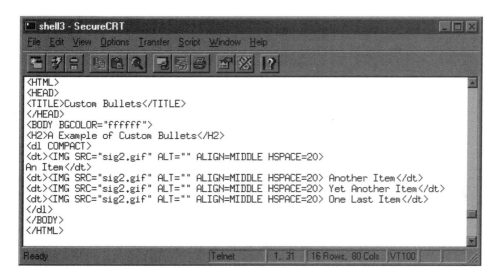

LAB 4.4 SELF-REVIEW QUESTIONS

1) An example of an ordered list is
   a) A grocery list
   b) A to-do list
   c) A step-by-step set of instructions

2) Unordered list items are, by default, preceded by
   a) Letters
   b) Numbers
   c) Bullets

3) The default bullet for an unordered list is a
   a) Disc
   b) Square
   c) Circle

4) The correct code to start an ordered list with the lower-case letter m is
   a) `<OL START="m" TYPE="A">`
   b) `<OL START="13">`
   c) `<OL START="13" TYPE="a">`
   d) It can't be done

Quiz answers appear in the Appendix, Section 4.4.

L A B   4 . 5

THREE IMAGE ATTRIBUTES

In the previous two chapters, you learned about including an image on a Web page and a few of the <IMG> element's attributes. In this section, we will take the element a bit further, learning how to position an image on a page, as well as how to format text around it.

Examine Figures 4.8, 4.9, and 4.10. Notice how the content of the Web page is the same as found in Figure 3.8. A careful look at the HTML code reveals how the introduction of just a few attributes can dramatically alter the appearance of a page that contains images and text.

The ALIGN attribute is used to either position an image at the left or right margin of a page or to position text at the top, middle, or bottom of the image. When the value of ALIGN is LEFT or RIGHT, as shown in Figures 4.9 and 4.10, the image is shifted to the left or right side of the page

```
<HTML>
<HEAD>
<!-- A very simple HTML example for the Prentice Hall book. -->
<TITLE>Arlyn has a cat named Fitch</TITLE>
</HEAD>

<BODY>
<H1>I have a cat named Fitch</H1>

<IMG SRC="fitchlitlit.gif" ALT="This is a picture of Fitch, a black & white
domestic longhair." BORDER="14" ALIGN=LEFT VSPACE=25 HSPACE=15>

<P>
He has three roommates: Moreta, Amarina, and
Mamakin. Mamakin is the newest member of our household and came to us
```

Figure 4.8 ■ The coding of ALIGN, HSPACE, and VSPACE attributes.

Figure 4.9 ■ Left-aligning an image.

Figure 4.10 ■ Right-aligning an image.

Figure 4.11 ■ **IMG_SRC** with **ALIGN=TOP.**

Figure 4.12 ■ **IMG_SRC** with **ALIGN=MIDDLE.**

Figure 4.13 ■ **IMG_SRC with ALIGN=BOTTOM.**

accordingly and the text is wrapped around the image beginning at the top. Values of TOP, MIDDLE, or BOTTOM align the image to a single line of text as shown in Figures 4.11–4.13.

HSPACE and VSPACE, horizontal and vertical space, create margins around an image and are specified in pixels (see Figure 4.8). The default margin between an image and text is two pixels, which in most cases is not very appealing. Increasing the horizontal and vertical margins for your images will not only make your pages more attractive, but easier to read.

TURNING IMAGES INTO BUTTONS

Turning an image into a button that links to another page is quite simple and is an excellent example of how your pages can become more sophisticated as you become familiar with HTML elements, combining them to achieve desired effects. Figure 4.14 shows both the code that renders an image as a button and middle-aligned text that describes the link. Figure 4.15 is how Netscape displays the page. Note that an image button will by default have a blue border, the graphical indicator that an image is a button, around it. While you can eliminate this border by setting the BORDER attribute to zero (BORDER=0), it isn't recommended as your visitors will not immediately know that the graphic is a button and, unless you include a text link as well, may never visit the related page or site.

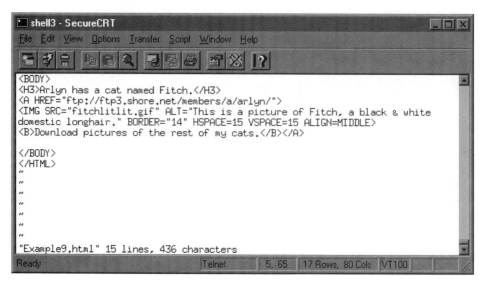

Figure 4.14 ■ Coding a button.

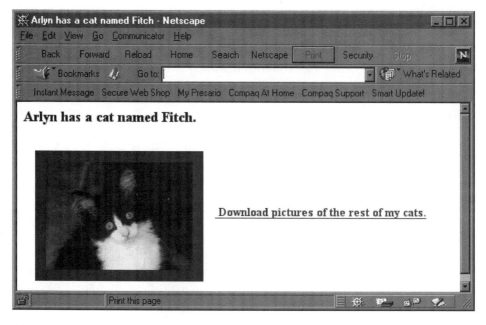

Figure 4.15 ■ An image button in Netscape.

LAB 4.5 EXERCISES

4.5.1 THREE IMAGE ATTRIBUTES

a) Using `fitchlitlit.gif` as your image, write the code that will produce the following effects:

  1) The image is centered with text centered above and below it.

_____

_____

  2) The image is aligned to the right with a 40-pixel border and a 20-pixel margin. Text wraps around the image.

_____

_____

  3) Two copies of the image appear on the page, one aligned to the left and one aligned to the right. Text starts between the images.

_____

_____

LAB
4.5

b) Keeping in mind that images are inline elements, reproduce the following page:

LAB 4.5 EXERCISE ANSWERS

4.5.1 ANSWERS

a) Using `fitchlitlit.gif` as your image, write the code that will produce the following effects:

1) The image is centered with text centered above and below it.

Answer:

```
<HTML>
<HEAD>
<!-- A very simple HTML example for the Prentice Hall book. -->
<TITLE>Arlyn has a cat named Fitch</TITLE>
</HEAD>

<BODY>
<CENTER>
<H1>I have a cat named Fitch</H1>

<IMG SRC="fitchlitlit.gif" ALT="This is a picture of Fitch, a black & white
domestic longhair." BORDER="14" HSPACE=25>
<BR>
<P>
He has three roommates: Moreta, Amarina, and
Mamakin. Mamakin is the newest member of our household and came to us
with four kittens in tow, all of which we were lucky enough to find homes
for.
</P>
<UL>
<LI><A HREF="http://cats.about.com/">All About Cats</A>
<LI><A HREF="ftp://ftp.shore.net/members1/a/arlyn/">Grab pictures of my cats</A>
<BR><BR>
<LI><A HREF="mailto:arlyn@shore.net">Send me mail</A>
<LI><A HREF="http://www.shore.net/~arlyn/siteindex.html">Return to my Index Page
</A>
</UL>
</CENTER>
</BODY>
</HTML>
"answer4_4a1.html" 29 lines, 831 characters
```

**LAB
4.5**

2) The image is aligned to the right with a 40-pixel border and a 20-pixel margin. Text wraps around the image.

Answer:

3) Two copies of the image appear on the page, one aligned to the left and one aligned to the right. Text starts between the images.

Answer:

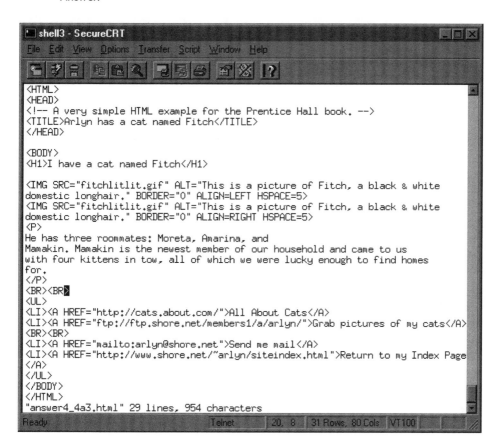

b) Keeping in mind that images are inline elements, reproduce the following page:

Answer:

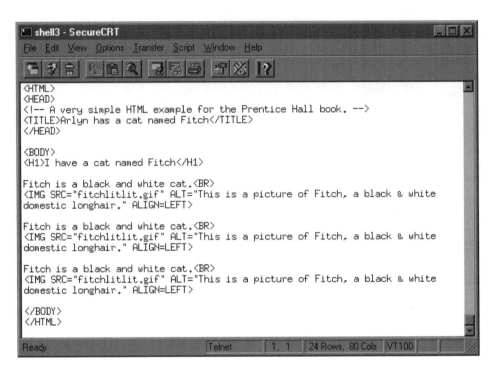

LAB 4.5 SELF-REVIEW QUESTIONS

1) The default margin around an image is
   a) 0 pixels
   b) 2 pixels
   c) 5 pixels

2) The default placement for an image is
   a) In line with document content
   b) Aligned to the left
   c) Aligned to the right

3) ALIGN=TOP aligns
   a) The image to the top of the document
   b) The image to the top of a paragraph
   c) The image's top to a single line of text

4) `ALIGN=LEFT` aligns
   a) The image to the left and text follows the image
   b) The text to the left and the image follows the text
   c) The image to the left and text wraps around the image

5) The `VSPACE` attribute is used to adjust all four margins of an image.
   a) True
   b) False

6) An image used as a button will have a border by default.
   a) True
   b) False

Quiz answers appear in the Appendix, Section 4.5.

L A B   4 . 6

BODY COLOR AND BACKGROUND ATTRIBUTES

Now that we have covered the bulk of the generic HTML elements, we can proceed with more of their attributes. In this section, we will cover BODY element attributes, which will allow you to further customize the appearance of your Web pages.

Why, you might ask, weren't these attributes discussed earlier? The philosophy followed here is, "Basics first." It is all too easy to lose sight of the function of a Web page and its contents if one gets caught up in its design aspects. Now that you have a good handle on the function of the various HTML elements, we can look at a few more attributes.

**LAB
4.6**

First, a note to the wise. Use these attributes sparingly and with care. More than one Web page designer has been guilty of going overboard with customizing Web pages to the point of rendering them unattractive and/or unusable. Once again, think about why you are overriding the default characteristics of your page and consider the reaction of your visitors to your choices. Two cliches apply perfectly here:

Less is more.

and

All things in moderation.

Please take them to heart.

BACKGROUND COLORS AND BACKGROUND IMAGES

Page backdrops can be a nice touch and add a lot to the overall mood of your site. On the other hand, there is a reason why books are published using black text on white pages. It is never acceptable to sacrifice the readability of your Web pages in favor of wild colors and backgrounds.

It should also be noted that the use of background images can add significantly to the time that it takes to download your page. If you use them, make your best effort to keep the size of the image file small.

BGCOLOR   Background Color

EXAMPLE:

```
<BODY BGCOLOR="#ffffff">
Or
<BODY BGCOLOR="white"
```

```
<BODY BGCOLOR="#000000">
Or
<BODY BGCOLOR="black">
```

The background color of a page can be set using a color's RGB (red, green, and blue) or hexadecimal value, or a color name. In most cases, it is best to use RGB values, as the browsers will produce more accurate colors.

BACKGROUND   Background image

EXAMPLE:

```
<BODY BACKGROUND="selfport2.jpg">
```

Here, an image called `selfport2.jpg` will be used as the background for this particular Web page. Note that smaller images will tile, or repeat themselves, until the background is filled. As you can well imagine, this could make for impossibly busy backgrounds if one is not careful.

Unless you want your background to default to the visitor's choice of color, it is a good idea when specifying a background image to include a background color to be used in the event that the image cannot be displayed. See Figures 4.16 and 4.17 for sample code and the resulting page. Note how `selfport2.jpg` starts to repeat itself.

**LAB
4.6**

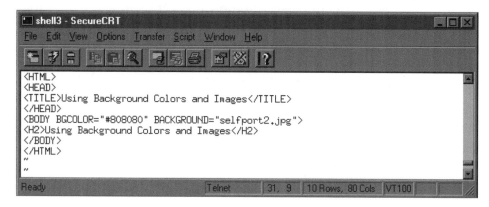

Figure 4.16 ■ **Using background images.**

```
<HTML>
<HEAD>
<TITLE>Using Background Colors and Images</TITLE>
</HEAD>
<BODY BGCOLOR="#808080" BACKGROUND="selfport2.jpg">
<H2>Using Background Colors and Images</H2>
</BODY>
</HTML>
~
~
```

Figure 4.17 ■ **The HTML code for Figure 4.16.**

TEXT COLORS

If you set the background color or image of your Web page, it is a very good idea to set the text colors, and vice versa. In most cases, this will prevent a visitor's browser preferences from rendering the text on your page invisible. Imagine, for example, the results if you set your background color to blue without setting an appropriate text color and your visitor's text defaults to the same shade of blue. Or, how would a visitor-set text color of red look on your blue page?

Other factors to consider are:

- **Color-blindness**—A large number of people are color-blind and are not able to see certain color combinations. Red and green used together is an example.
- **Display capabilities**—Not all colors will be available on all displays, and when the exact color is not found, the display will use the closest match it can find. This can lead to illegible and unattractive results.
- **Personal preferences**—What might be a beautiful color scheme to you may completely alienate a visitor. It is best to stick with standard or conservative color combinations.
- **Color implications**—Many colors carry immediate messages to the individual: red means danger or stop, yellow means caution, and green means go in the western world. Colors can also be grouped into cool (blue, green, and violet) and warm (red, orange, and yellow), and will have certain effects on your visitors when used. In the world of the Web, blue means a link has not been visited and purple means it has. Be aware of how colors speak to people and be careful about breaking accepted conventions.

**LAB
4.6**

Once you have given careful thought to your text color scheme, there are a number of attributes available.

TEXT   Text color

EXAMPLE:

<BODY BGCOLOR="blue" TEXT="yellow">

In this example, the background color is set to blue and the text color to yellow, a rather intense combination for any extended reading.

LINK TEXT	LINK	Unvisited link
	ALINK	Active link – A link just as it is clicked
	VLINK	An already visited link

EXAMPLE:

```
<BODY BGCOLOR="white" LINK="green" ALINK=
"orange" VLINK="red">
```

LAB 4.6 EXERCISE

4.6.1   BODY COLOR AND BACKGROUND ATTRIBUTES

Think about the Web site that you want to create. Come up with several color combinations and background selections that appeal to you and make sense as part of your design. Write the HTML code for a simple page and review it with a browser to see if the color scheme is still appealing. If it is, ask someone else to look at the page and critique your choices.

LAB 4.6 SELF-REVIEW QUESTIONS

1)   All colors are understood and displayed uniformly on all platforms.
    a) True
    b) False

2)   The preferred method of setting a color is using the
    a) Color name
    b) RGB or hexadecimal value

3)   Background images that are not large enough to fill a browser window will
    a) Automatically resize to fill the window
    b) Appear in the center of the window
    c) Tile until the window is filled

4)   When setting the background color for a Web page, one should always
    a) Set all other pages to the same color
    b) Set the color to white
    c) Set the text color

5)   Users have the ability to set background and text colors with their browsers.
    a) True
    b) False

6) Background images
   a) Slow down page downloads
   b) May tile in unexpected ways
   c) May detract from the readability of a page
   d) All of the above

Quiz answers appear in the Appendix, Section 4.6.

**LAB
4.6**

CHAPTER 4

TEST YOUR THINKING

The projects in this section use the skills you've acquired in this chapter. The answers to these projects are available to instructors only through a Prentice Hall sales representative and are intended to be used in classroom discussion and assessment.

At this point, you should be familiar with all of the simple HTML elements and their attributes. Return to the pages you created at the end of Chapter 3 and incorporate applicable elements you learned in this chapter.

1) Add more images to the pages and experiment with various alignments, and how they affect how the page is read.

2) Add a large image (one that will fill a browser window) as a background and test the download time for the pages. Change the image to a smaller one that will tile and critically review the readability of the pages.

3) Experiment with different background/text color combinations and note how they change the mood of your pages. Suggestions:

  a) red text on a black background

  b) purple text on a yellow background

  c) brown text on a beige background

CHAPTER 5

TABLES

 Now go, write it before them in a table. . . .

The Bible
Isaiah 30:7–8

CHAPTER OBJECTIVES

In this chapter, you will learn about:

✔ The anatomy of a table	Page 111
✔ Basic table elements and attributes	Page 114
✔ Additional table elements and attributes	Page 122
✔ Using tables to format Web pages	Page 132
✔ Nested tables	Page 136

Table elements were first introduced on the Web as a means of organizing tabular information in a more sophisticated manner than could previously be achieved through the use of the <PRE> element. HTML authors now had the ability to create borders of different widths and colors, include images in table cells, and vary the font style and weight of table content.

It was not long, however, before Web designers stumbled on to the idea of using tables to produce highly formatted Web pages. Until tables came onto the scene, designers had to depend on the fairly simple formatting elements that came with HTML, filling space with invisible images to achieve exact formatting. Tables gave designers a way to divide a Web page into a grid into which they could place their content.

To the HTML purist, this was a bit of an affront. It was not the manner in which tables were **intended** to be used. But, it **is** a perfect example of how people will push the envelope with the tools they are given, going beyond the tool's original intent.

L A B   5 . 1

THE ANATOMY
OF A TABLE

Tables, not unlike the lists you worked with in Chapter 4, are a system of HTML elements used to create a specially formatted whole. They represent probably the most code-intensive aspect of HTML, save style sheets, which will be described later in the book, and careful attention needs to be paid to your starting and ending elements. Tables are also a perfect example of when it is absolutely necessary to set your personal code style early; as discussed in Chapter 3, for the sake of readability and to include comments to let you and anyone else know what a block of code is doing.

All that said, take a look at the following table source code and, based on what you have learned about HTML elements and attributes in the previous chapters, see if you can guess what the end result might look like. Then see Figure 5.1 for the actual page.

```
<HTML>
<HEAD>
<TITLE>A Simple Table</TITLE>
</HEAD>
<BODY BGCOLOR="ffffff" TEXT="000000">
<H2>A Simple Table</H2>
<TABLE  CELLSPACING=1 CELLPADDING=5>
<CAPTION ALIGN=BOTTOM>
Arlyn has four cats.
</CAPTION>
<TR>
    <TH>Name</TH><TH>Age</TH><TH>Color</TH><TH>See a
Picture?</TH>
</TR>
<TR>
    <TD>Moreta</TD><TD>15</TD><TD>Calico</TD><TD><A
HREF="moreta.jpg">Yes</A></TD>
</TR>
<TR>
```

```
    <TD>Fitch</TD><TD>3</TD><TD>Black &
White</TD><TD><A HREF="fitchlit.gif">Yes</A></TD>
</TR>
<TR>
    <TD>Amarina</TD><TD>3</TD><TD>Peach</TD><TD><A
HREF="amabig.jpg">Yes</A></TD>
</TR>
<TR>

<TD>Mamakin</TD><TD>1</TD><TD>White</TD><TD>No</TD>
</TR>
</TABLE>
</BODY>
```

Notice how the row containing information about Fitch is taller than the other three. Cell and row sizes, unless specifically set in pixels, will expand and contract as needed depending on the size of the browser window. The exact same table is displayed in Figure 5.2 after widening the browser window just a bit.

This is, in many ways, a very nice feature of tables in that a user has a good chance of being able to see your entire table without scrolling or resizing the browser window. On the other hand, it modifies the appearance of your table, which, in some cases, may not be a desirable thing.

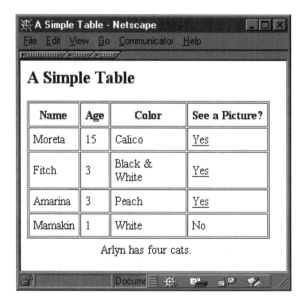

Figure 5.1 ■ A simple table.

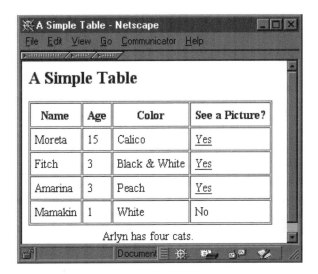

Figure 5.2 ■ A simple table, widened.

L A B   5 . 2

BASIC TABLE ELEMENTS AND ATTRIBUTES

There are only five main table elements, which makes the creation of simple tables very easy. On the other hand, there are numerous attributes associated with each element. The trick to learning tables is to go slowly, add fancier attributes after you've mastered the basics, and to keep your code clear. Nothing will hinder you in working with tables as much as code that is difficult to read.

TABLE

As we have seen with most other elements, `<TABLE>` and `</TABLE>` signal the beginning and end of the desired format. While working with tables, you will notice that the omission of either element will produce some pretty drastic results:

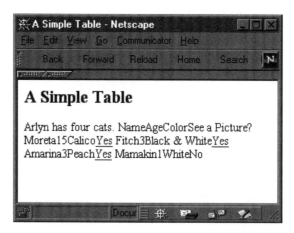

Figure 5.3 ■ A table with no `<TABLE>`.

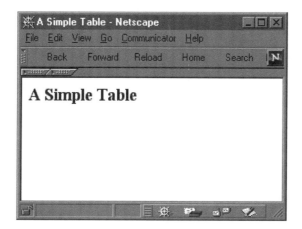

Figure 5.4 ■ A table with no </TABLE>.

The reason this is mentioned here is that finding the errors that generate the pages in Figures 5.3 and 5.4 is not entirely intuitive until you become fairly fluent with table code. Even then, it is almost guaranteed that you will be stung with the above situations once in a while and spend more time than you'd like debugging your elements.

The TABLE element can take a number of attributes.

> **ALIGN**—The ALIGN attribute for the TABLE element specifies where the table should be placed horizontally on the page. By default, if ALIGN is not set, a table will appear flush to the left and text will appear above and below it. The values for ALIGN are:

> **LEFT** Position the table against the left margin and let text flow around the right side.
>
> > **Example:** <TABLE ALIGN=LEFT>

> **CENTER** Center the table on the page with text flowing above and below it.
>
> > **Example:** <TABLE ALIGN=CENTER>

> **RIGHT** Position the table against the right margin and let text flow around the left side.
>
> > **Example:** <TABLE ALIGN=RIGHT>

BACKGROUND—Specifies a background image for the table, which will override that of the body background if it has been used. The value of BACKGROUND is an image file. This attribute is particularly effective with a borderless table.

Example: <TABLE BACKGROUND="image.gif">

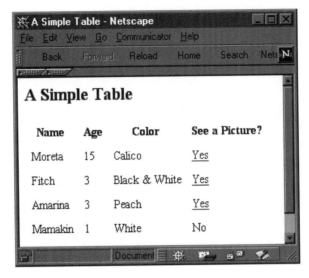

Figure 5.5 ■ A borderless table.

BGCOLOR—Specifies the background color for a table. Colors may be indicated as either names or RGB values.

Example: <TABLE BGCOLOR="red">

or

<TABLE BGCOLOR="#ff0000">

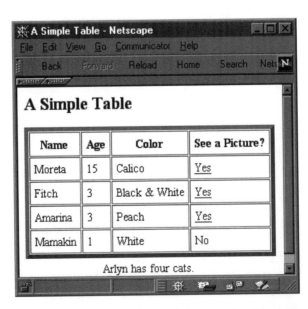

Figure 5.6 ■ A table with a 5-pixel border.

BORDER—The default border for a table has a width of 1. Including the BORDER attribute in a TABLE element turns borders on as seen in Figure 5.6. Setting the value of BORDER in pixels can increase a table's border width. Observe the effects of changing the BORDER attribute for the table in Figure 5.1.

Example: <TABLE> (No border—Figure 5.5)

               <TABLE BORDER=5> (A 5-pixel border—Figure 5.6)

BORDERCOLOR—Changes the color of the table border when the BORDER attribute is set. The color may be specified as either a name or an RGB value.

Example: <TABLE BORDER=5 BORDERCOLOR="red">

CELLPADDING—Indicates the number of pixels between a table cell's interior edge and its contents. The default spacing is one pixel. Setting the spacing to 0 will cause the contents of the cell to touch the cell edge.

Example: <TABLE   CELLPADDING=5>

CELLSPACING—Indicates the number of pixels between cells.

Example: <TABLE   CELLPADDING=5 CELLSPACING=1>

The values for CELLPADDING and CELLSPACING are 5 and 1, respectively for the table in Figure 5.1. Figure 5.7 illustrates what happens to the appearance of our table when those values are reversed.

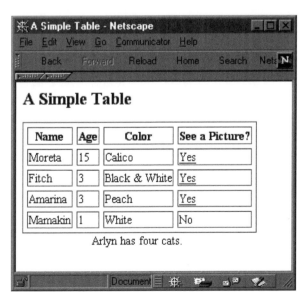

Figure 5.7 ■ **CELLPADDING=1 and CELLSPACING=5.**

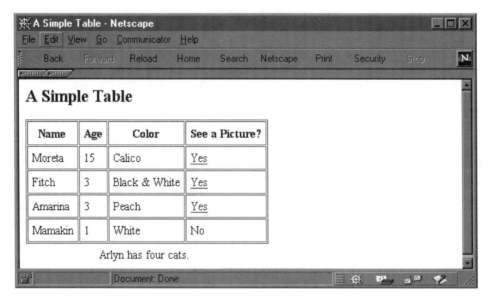

Figure 5.8 ■ The table with no `WIDTH` set.

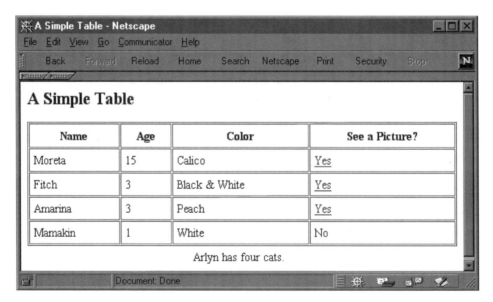

Figure 5.9 ■ The table with `WIDTH="100%"`.

WIDTH—Sets the width of a table as either a percentage of the browser window (this can actually be greater than 100%) or a number of pixels. By default, a browser will only render a table as large as it needs to be to display all of its contents. Returning again to the table in Figure 5.1, notice how increasing the size of the browser window does not affect the size of the table since the WIDTH attribute has not been set (Figure 5.8). If, however, we set the table's width to 100%, the table size will increase to fill the width of the browser window as can be seen in Figure 5.9.

Example: <TABLE CELLSPACING=1 CELLPADDING=5
WIDTH="100%">

LAB 5.2 EXERCISES

5.2.1 BASIC TABLE ELEMENTS AND ATTRIBUTES

The TABLE element for the table in Figure 5.1 is:

```
<TABLE   CELLSPACING=1 CELLPADDING=5>
```

Modify the element to achieve the following effects:

a) A table with no border and `fitchlit.gif` as a background image.

_____

_____

b) A table with a blue, 10-pixel border.

_____

_____

c) A table with no borders.

_____

_____

d) A table whose cells are 8 pixels apart.

_____

_____

e) A table whose cells' contents are separated from the cell borders by 1 pixel.

_____

_____

f) A table that fills 60% of the browser window and has a yellow background.

_____

_____

g) A table that is positioned at the right-hand side of the browser.

_____

_____

LAB 5.2 EXERCISE ANSWERS

5.2.1 ANSWERS

The TABLE element for the table in Figure 5.1 is:

```
<TABLE CELLSPACING=1 CELLPADDING=5>
```

Modify the element to achieve the following effects.

a) A table with no border and `fitchlit.gif` as a background image.

Answer: `<TABLE BACKGROUND="fitchlit.gif>`

b) A table with a blue, 10-pixel border.

Answer: `<TABLE BORDER=10>`

c) A table with no borders.

Answer: <TABLE>

d) A table whose cells are 8 pixels apart.

Answer: <TABLE CELLSPACING=8>

e) A table whose cells' contents are separated from the cell borders by 1 pixel.

Answer: <TABLE CELLPADDING=1>

f) A table that fills 60% of the browser window and has a yellow background.

Answer: <TABLE WIDTH=60% BGCOLOR="yellow">

g) A table that is positioned at the right-hand side of the browser.

Answer: <TABLE ALIGN=RIGHT>

LAB 5.2 SELF-REVIEW QUESTIONS

1) By default, a browser will display a table as:
   a) 100% of the browser window
   b) Large as it needs to be to include all of the table's contents

2) By default, a table will be aligned
   a) Flush left with text above and below
   b) Centered with text above and below
   c) Flush right with text above and below

3) Tables were **originally** intended to be used as a means of
   a) Formatting Web pages
   b) Presenting tabular data

Quiz answers appear in the Appendix, Section 5.2.

L A B   5 . 3

ADDITIONAL
TABLE ELEMENTS
AND ATTRIBUTES

TH

The TH element creates headers for your table columns. By default, browsers will render header text bold and centered. TH accepts all of the same attributes as the TD element, which is discussed later.

THEAD

THEAD specifies a number of rows as a header for a table that will repeat if the table crosses page boundaries. Only one THEAD may occur within a single table.

TFOOT

TFOOT designates a number of rows as a table footer that will repeat if the table crosses page boundaries. Only one TFOOT may occur within a single table.

TBODY

TBODY is used to separate a table into sections with a horizontal rule. Any number of sections or groups can be created using TBODY elements.

COLGROUP

Just as the name of the element implies, COLGROUP is used to group table columns together. It, along with the COL element, is recognized by HTML 4.0-compliant browsers and should therefore be used with some care. The following code example illustrates the use of COLGROUP and the SPAN attribute to define a set of five columns.

```
<COLGROUP SPAN=2 WIDTH="60%" ALIGN=left>
<COLGROUP SPAN=3 WIDTH="40%" ALIGN=right>
```

The first column group contains two columns and will fill 60% of the table width. The second column group contains three columns and fills the remaining 40% of the table. The ALIGN attribute sets the position of content for all of the columns within each group.

COL

The COL element can be used if columns within a single COLGROUP need to have different attributes. For instance:

```
<COLGROUP SPAN=2 WIDTH="60%" ALIGN=left>
<COLGROUP WIDTH="40%">
<COL ALIGN=center SPAN=2>
<COL ALIGN=right>
```

Again, the code defines five columns. The first group contains two columns with content aligned to the left. The second group contains three columns, two that have content center-aligned, and the last with content aligned to the right. When COL is used, the SPAN attribute should not be included in COLGROUP as browsers will ignore COL elements that follow.

CAPTION

CAPTION labels content you wish to use as a sort of title or explanatory line for your table. By default, the caption will appear centered at the top of the table, but you may move it to the bottom of the table with the ALIGN attribute as such: ALIGN=BOTTOM.

TR

TR causes a new row to be inserted into a table. The element takes a number of attributes that affect the appearance of all the cells within a given row. These effects can be overridden within an individual cell, as you will see in the discussion of the TD element later. Assume that the syntax for the attributes and their values are the same as were shown for the TABLE element unless specified otherwise.

ALIGN—Formats content horizontally in a row's cells. There are four values that can be used in conjunction with ALIGN:

LEFT   Left-justified content, the default.

RIGHT   Right-justified content.

CENTER   Centered content.

JUSTIFY Left- and right-justified content.

VALIGN—Formats content vertically in a row's cells. The values assigned to VALIGN are:

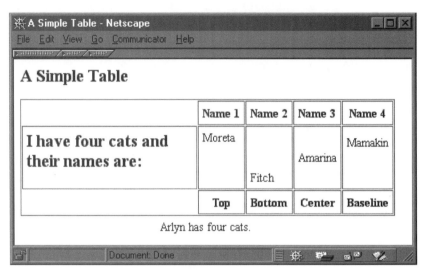

Figure 5.10 ■ **VALIGN illustrated.**

TOP	Aligned flush against the top of the cells.
BOTTOM	Aligned flush against the bottom of the cells.
CENTER	Aligned in the center of the cells, the default.
BASELINE	Aligned to another cell's first line of text.

See Figure 5.10 for a demonstration of how the VALIGN attribute and its different values affect the position of text in a row of table cells.

BGCOLOR—Sets the background color for a row of cells.

BORDERCOLOR—Sets the border color for a row of cells.

TD

TD delineates the contents of your data cells. Unless specified with attributes, browsers will automatically size data cells to accommodate both the text they contain and the size of the browser window. Also, unless handled with attributes, every row will have the same number of cells whether or not you provide content for them.

TD and TH take on many of the same attributes as TABLE and TR, as well as a couple of new ones.

ALIGN—Used to align content horizontally in a table cell. The values and behaviors of the attribute are the same as those when ALIGN is used with the TR element.

VALIGN—Used to align content vertically in a table cell. Again, the same values and behaviors of VALIGN when used with TR apply.

HEIGHT—Specifies the height of a table cell either as a percentage of the browser window or in pixels. The height set will be interpreted to be the **minimum** size of the cell. If the browser needs more space to include all of the contents of any one cell, it will increase the height of the entire row as necessary.

WIDTH—Specifies the width of a table cell either as a percentage of the browser window or in pixels. As with the HEIGHT attribute, browsers will ignore this setting if a cell needs to be larger to display its data.

COLSPAN—Allows a cell to span, or cross, a number of columns. This attribute overrides the browser's inclination to display every row of a table with the same number of cells.

Example: `<TD COLSPAN=2>`

Figure 5.11 demonstrates the use of COLSPAN to force the first cell of each row to span the first two header columns.

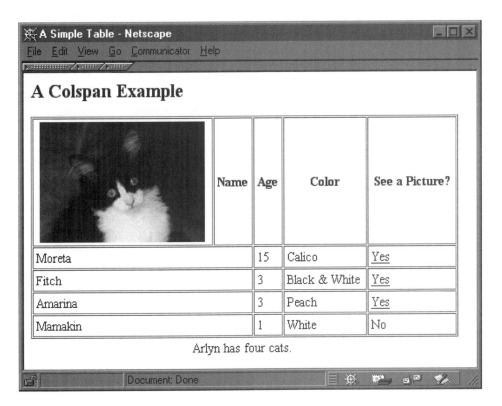

Figure 5.11 ■ A table with COLSPAN=2.

ROWSPAN—Allows a cell to span, or cross, a number of rows.

Example: `<TH ROWSPAN=5>`

Figure 5.12 shows the table with `ROWSPAN=5` in the `TH` cell containing the image rather than forcing the first cell of subsequent rows to span two columns. Note how, for the purposes of including a picture, the `ROWSPAN` attribute produces more aesthetically pleasing results.

BGCOLOR—Used to set the background color of a table cell.

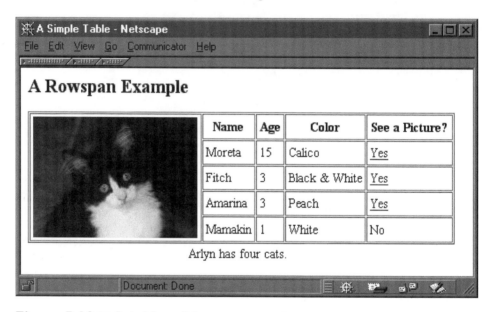

Figure 5.12 ■ **A table with ROWSPAN=5.**

LAB 5.3 EXERCISES

5.3.1 ADDITIONAL TABLE ELEMENTS AND ATTRIBUTES

The table examples we have looked at so far have been fairly simple. Tables can, however, get quite complicated as attributes are used to change the size and appearance of cells.

a) Examine the following table source code and draw the resulting table.

```
<HTML>
<HEAD>
<TITLE>A Slightly More Complicated Table</TITLE>
</HEAD>
<BODY BGCOLOR="ffffff" TEXT="000000">
<H2>A Slightly More Complicated Table</H2>
<TABLE  CELLSPACING=1 CELLPADDING=5 WIDTH="100%">
<CAPTION ALIGN=TOP>
<H3>Arlyn has four cats.</H3>
</CAPTION>
<TR BGCOLOR="lightblue">

     <TH>Name</TH><TH>Age</TH><TH>Color</TH><TH>Com-
ments</TH>
</TR>
<TR>

     <TD>Moreta</TD><TD>15</TD><TD>Calico</TD><TD>She
sheds!</TD>
</TR>
<TR>
     <TD>Fitch</TD><TD ROWSPAN=2>3</TD><TD>Black &
White</TD><TD ROWSPAN=2>Fitch and Amarina<BR> are
brother and sister.</TD>
</TR>
<TR>
     <TD>Amarina</TD><TD>Peach</TD>
</TR>
<TR>
     <TD>Mamakin</TD><TD>1</TD><TD>White</TD> <TD>She
was a stray.</TD>
</TR>
```

```
<TR BGCOLOR="#000000">
<TD COLSPAN=2><BR></TD><TD><IMG
SRC="fitchlitlit.gif"></TD><TD><BR></TD>
</TR>
</TABLE>
</BODY>
</HTML>
```

b) The following table uses quite a few, perhaps too many, table attributes. Write the code that might render this table.

Two clues: 1. Use <BR> as a placeholder in empty cells.
2. The size of this table is not a function of the browser.

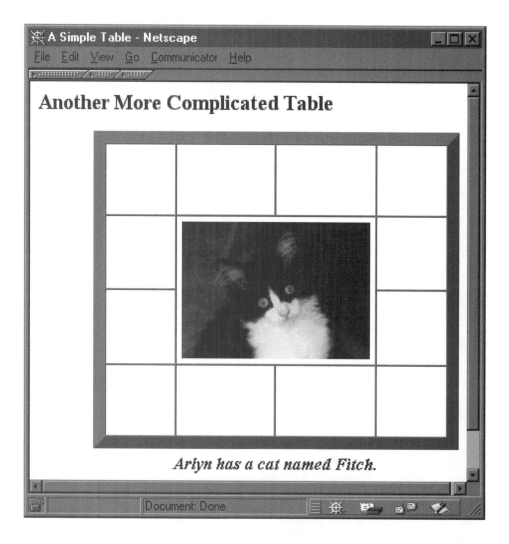

LAB 5.3 EXERCISE ANSWERS

a) Examine the following table source code and draw the resulting table.

Answer: Netscape renders the listed code as follows:

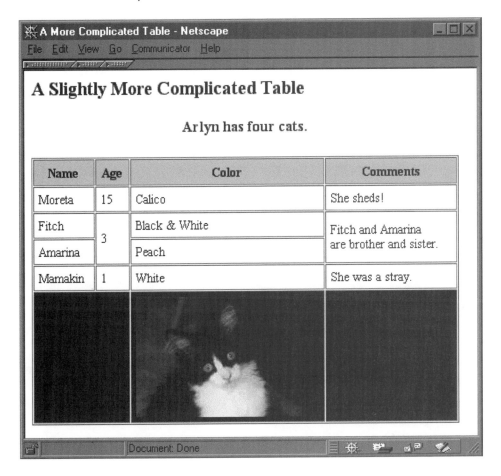

b) The following table uses quite a few, perhaps too many, table attributes. Write the code that might render this table.

Answer: The code for the table in this exercise is:

```
<HTML>
<HEAD>
<TITLE>Another More Complicated Table</TITLE>
</HEAD>
<BODY BGCOLOR="ffffff" TEXT="000000">
<H2>Another More Complicated Table</H2>
<TABLE BORDER=12 CELLSPACING=0 CELLPADDING=5
ALIGN=RIGHT>
<CAPTION ALIGN=BOTTOM>
<H3><I>Arlyn has a cat named Fitch.</I></H3>
</CAPTION>
<TR>
<TD HEIGHT=60
WIDTH=60><BR></TD><TD><BR></TD><TD><BR></TD><TD
WIDTH=60><BR></TD>
</TR>
<TR>
<TD><BR></TD><TD COLSPAN=2 ROWSPAN=2><IMG SRC="fitch-
litlit.gif"></TD><TD><BR></TD>
</TD>
<TR>
<TD><BR></TD><TD><BR></TD>
</TR>
<TR>
<TD
HEIGHT=60><BR></TD><TD><BR></TD><TD><BR></TD><TD><BR>
</TD>
</TR>
</TABLE>
</BODY>
</HTML>
```

LAB 5.3 SELF-REVIEW QUESTIONS

1) Table data cells may contain
   a) Text
   b) Links
   c) Images
   d) Tables
   e) All of the above

2) If not specified with size attributes, browsers will make data cells
   a) Equal in size
   b) Of differing sizes according to cell content

3) When specified, the HEIGHT and WIDTH attributes specify the
   a) minimum
   b) absolute
   c) maximum
   size of a data cell.

4) The COLSPAN attribute specifies
   a) The width of a column in pixels
   b) The width of a column in number of columns

5) By default, the CAPTION for a table will appear
   a) Aligned left, above the table
   b) Aligned center, above the table
   c) Aligned left, below the table
   d) Aligned center, below the table

6) The width of a table can be set to be larger than the browser window.
   a) True
   b) False

7) The default padding for a table cell is
   a) 0 pixels
   b) 1 pixel
   c) 5 pixels

8) The background color can be set for
   a) An entire table
   b) A table row
   c) A table cell
   d) All of the above

Quiz answers appear in the Appendix, Section 5.3.

L A B   5 . 4

USING TABLES TO FORMAT WEB PAGES

As mentioned in the introduction to this chapter, it didn't take long for Web designers to conclude that borderless tables were an excellent way to format a Web page. While the new HTML standards encourage the use of style sheets to do this, many interesting effects can be achieved using a table's rows and cells to position the various elements of a Web page. Additionally, as seen in Exercise 5.2.b, a table can be an interesting means of presenting an image.

Consider the Web page in Figure 5.13, which has three columns of text, each containing a chapter introduction from this book:

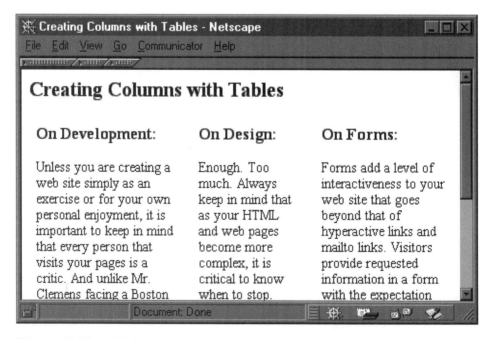

Figure 5.13 ■ Using a table to produce text columns.

The source code for the page (minus the actual content text) is very simple:

```
<HTML>
<HEAD>
<TITLE>Creating Columns with Tables</TITLE>
</HEAD>
<BODY BGCOLOR="ffffff" TEXT="000000">
<H2>Creating Columns with Tables</H2>
<TABLE CELLSPACING=0 CELLPADDING=5>
<TR>
<TD VALIGN=TOP>
...
</TD>
<TD WIDTH=10><BR></TD>
<TD VALIGN=TOP>
...
</TD>
<TD WIDTH=10><BR></TD>
<TD VALIGN=TOP>
```

Creating Side Headers with Tables

On Development:	Unless you are creating a web site simply as an exercise or for your own personal enjoyment, it is important to keep in mind that every person that visits your pages is a critic. And unlike Mr. Clemens facing a Boston audience, 4000 critics, you are facing the Internet, millions of critics. Hence, it is wise to think a web site through on a number of different levels prior to beginning the coding of pages.
On Design:	Enough. Too much. Always keep in mind that as your HTML and web pages become more complex, it is critical to know when to stop. You will learn about a number of ways to format and customize your web pages in this chapter but remember, *"Just because you can doesn't mean you do."*
On Forms:	Forms add a level of interactiveness to your web site that goes beyond that of hyperactive links and mailto links. Visitors provide requested information in a form with the expectation of receiving something in return be it merchandise, information, or simply a response. The form is a vehicle for true give and take between a web site visitor and the site owner.

Figure 5.14 ■ **Using a table to create side headers.**

```
...
</TD>
</TR>
</TABLE>
</BODY>
</HTML>
```

The entire page is a table with one row of five cells. Three of the cells hold the text of the documents. The other two serve as separators between the text columns.

Another popular trick is to use tables to create side headers, or sidebars for paragraphs of text. Figure 5.14 shows the table in Figure 5.13 rewritten in this fashion.

LAB 5.4

LAB 5.4 EXERCISE

5.4.1 USING TABLES TO FORMAT WEB PAGES

Examine the page in Figure 5.14 and think about the table elements that you would use to produce the page. Write the code.

LAB 5.4 EXERCISE ANSWER

5.4.1 ANSWER

Examine the page in Figure 5.14 and think about the table elements that you would use to produce the page. Write the code.

Answer: The code (minus the paragraph text) for the Web page in Figure 5.14 is:

```
<HTML>
<HEAD>
<TITLE>Creating Side Headers with Tables</TITLE>
</HEAD>
<BODY BGCOLOR="ffffff" TEXT="000000">
<H2>Creating Side Headers with Tables</H2>
<TABLE CELLSPACING=0 CELLPADDING=5>
<TR>
<TD VALIGN=CENTER>
<H3>On Development:</H3>
</TD>
<TD>
```

```
...
<BR>
</TD>
</TR>
<TR>
<TD VALIGN=CENTER>
<H3>On Design:</H3>
</TD>
<TD>

...
<BR>
</TD>
<TR>
<TD VALIGN=CENTER>
<H3>On Forms:</H3>
</TD>
<TD>

...
<BR>
</TD>
</TR>
</TABLE>
</BODY>
</HTML>
```

L A B   5 . 5

NESTED TABLES

It can be said without question that nested tables are probably the least favorite construct of HTML code for anyone learning to build Web pages. They can be difficult to sort out at first, and the code can get very messy, but if one is patient and treats the project as a bit of a puzzle, it can actually be enjoyable to put them together.

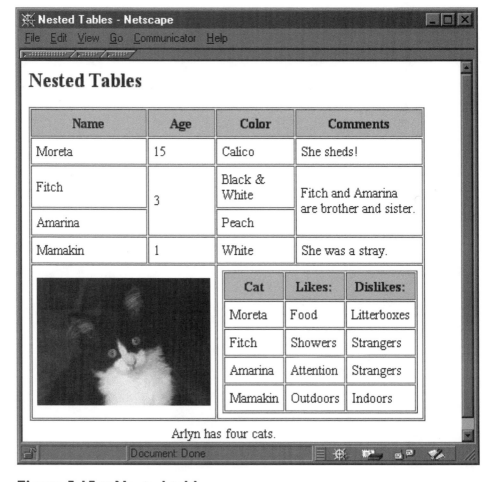

Figure 5.15 ■ Nested tables.

Put simply, a nested table is a table that resides inside another table. A sub-table replaces a cell in one table. Consider the table in Figure 5.15. Find the nested table and determine which cell, or cells, is holding it.

If you recall, this table is a modification of the one that appeared in Exercise 5.2.a. The changes that have been made are:

1) Row 4 has been divided into two cells, each of which span two columns.
2) The second cell of Row 4 has been filled with a new table.

The source code for the nested table, not including the code you already saw in Exercise 5.2.a is:

```
<TR>
<TD COLSPAN=2><IMG SRC="fitchlitlit.gif"></TD>
<TD COLSPAN=2>
        <TABLE  CELLSPACING=1 CELLPADDING=5"
WIDTH="100%">
        <TR BGCOLOR="lightblue">
                <TH>Cat</TH><TH>Likes:</TH><TH>
Dislikes:</TH>
        </TR>
        <TR>
                <TD>Moreta</TD><TD>Food</TD><TD>
Litterboxes</TD>
        </TR>
        <TR>

<TD>Fitch</TD><TD>Showers</TD><TD>Strangers</TD>
        </TR>
        <TR>

<TD>Amarina</TD><TD>Attention</TD><TD>Strangers</TD>
        </TR>
        <TR>

<TD>Mamakin</TD><TD>Outdoors</TD><TD>Indoors</TD>
        </TR>
        </TABLE>
</TD>
</TR>
</TABLE>
</BODY>
</HTML>
```

Note the lack of any magic here. The second cell of Row 4 contains nothing but elements and content for a very straightforward table.

LAB 5.5 EXERCISE

5.5.1 NESTED TABLES

Review the following Web page. How many tables does it contain? Write the source code for the page.

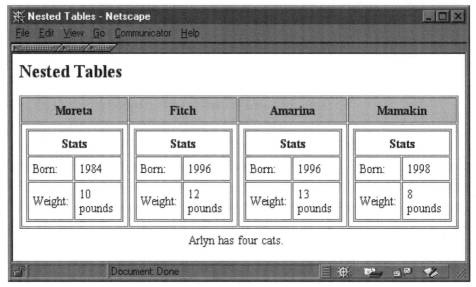

LAB 5.5 EXERCISE ANSWER

5.5.1 ANSWER

Review the following Web page. How many tables does it contain? Write the source code for the page.

Answer: The Web page contains five tables, a main table plus four nested tables. The source code for the entire page is:

```
<HTML>
<HEAD>
<TITLE>Nested Tables</TITLE>
</HEAD>
<BODY BGCOLOR="ffffff" TEXT="000000">
<H2>Nested Tables</H2>
```

```
<TABLE  CELLSPACING=1 CELLPADDING=5 WIDTH="75%">
<CAPTION ALIGN=BOTTOM>
Arlyn has four cats.
</CAPTION>
<TR BGCOLOR="lightblue">

        <TH>Moreta</TH><TH>Fitch</TH><TH>Amarina</TH>
<TH>Mamakin</TH>
</TR>
<TR>
    <TD>
        <TABLE  CELLSPACING=1 CELLPADDING=5
WIDTH="75%">
        <TR>
        <TH COLSPAN=2>Stats</TH>
        </TR>
        <TR>
        <TD>Born:</TD><TD>1984</TD>
        </TR>
        <TR>
        <TD>Weight:</TD><TD>10 pounds</TD>
        </TR>
        </TABLE>
    </TD>
<TD>
        <TABLE  CELLSPACING=1 CELLPADDING=5
WIDTH="75%">
        <TR>
        <TH COLSPAN=2>Stats</TH>
        </TR>
        <TR>
        <TD>Born:</TD><TD>1996</TD>
        </TR>
        <TR>
        <TD>Weight:</TD><TD>12 pounds</TD>
        </TR>
        </TABLE>
    </TD>
    <TD>
        <TABLE  CELLSPACING=1 CELLPADDING=5
WIDTH="75%">
        <TR>
        <TH COLSPAN=2>Stats</TH>
        </TR>
        <TR>
```

LAB
5.5

```
                    <TD>Born:</TD><TD>1996</TD>
                    </TR>
                    <TR>
                    <TD>Weight:</TD><TD>13 pounds</TD>
                    </TR>
                    </TABLE>
              </TD>
              <TD>
        <TABLE   CELLSPACING=1 CELLPADDING=5 WIDTH="75%">
                    <TR>
                    <TH COLSPAN=2>Stats</TH>
                    </TR>
                    <TR>
                    <TD>Born:</TD><TD>1998</TD>
                    </TR>
                    <TR>
                    <TD>Weight:</TD><TD>8 pounds</TD>
                    </TR>
                    </TABLE>
              </TD>
        </TR>
        </TABLE>
        </BODY>
        </HTML>
```

LAB 5.5 SELF-REVIEW QUESTION

1) A nested table is contained within a
   a) Table header
   b) Table row
   c) Table cell

Quiz answer appears in the Appendix, Section 5.5.

CHAPTER 5

TEST YOUR THINKING

The projects in this section use the skills you've acquired in this chapter. The answers to these projects are available to instructors only through a Prentice Hall sales representative and are intended to be used in classroom discussion and assessment.

Review the content of the Web site you are creating while working through these chapters and think of how tables might help you to present information in more interesting and efficient ways.

1) Create a table with three columns of text. The left column's text should be left-justified, the center's centered, and the right's right-justified.

2) Create a calendar containing a single month. Day numbers should be located in the bottom right corner of each day.

3) Use a table to format a page so that all of your primary links appear in a narrow left-hand column and your content appears in the right-hand column (this particular format is used in Chapter 8 where we talk about Server Side Includes).

Create a few tables of your own using as many of the elements and attributes you've learned about in this chapter as you can.

CHAPTER 6

FRAMES

 I had rather believe all the fables in the legends and the Talmud and the Alcoran, than that this universal frame is without a mind.

Francis Bacon
Apothegms (1624)

Never in the history of HTML has any other element been greeted with such intensity. While the BLINK element raised a bit of an uproar, it soon lost its place in the limelight. When frames first arrived on the scene, it seemed that the Web population immediately divided into two camps. There were those who loved frames, and sites appeared nearly overnight bearing the announcement that they were "Frames Only" and could only be viewed with "Frames-Capable Browsers." On the other side of the fence sat those who hated frames with a passion, some to the point of refusing to visit frames sites.

Fortunately, some of the intensity of feeling has died down, though there will always be someone who will summarily state, "I hate frames," when the element is mentioned. Still, they are to be used cautiously. Be certain, when you do use frames, that they make sense. The use of frames should add to, not detract from, the usability and performance of your site.

L A B 6 . 1

THE ANATOMY OF A FRAMES PAGE

When looking at a frames page, the important thing to know is that the HTML file for the page itself is actually a set of instructions for the display of several other HTML files. It can also be thought of as a container with multiple compartments, each one holding a single Web page. The frames

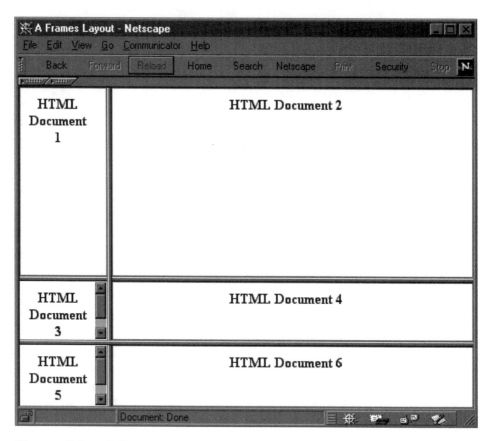

Figure 6.1 ■ A frames page.

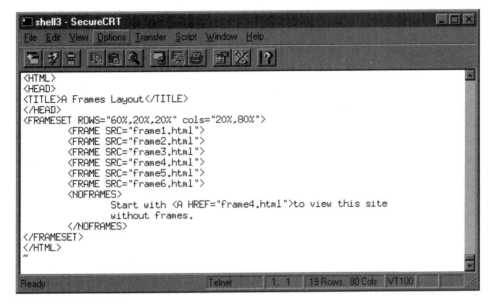

```
<HTML>
<HEAD>
<TITLE>A Frames Layout</TITLE>
</HEAD>
<FRAMESET ROWS="60%,20%,20%" cols="20%,80%">
        <FRAME SRC="frame1.html">
        <FRAME SRC="frame2.html">
        <FRAME SRC="frame3.html">
        <FRAME SRC="frame4.html">
        <FRAME SRC="frame5.html">
        <FRAME SRC="frame6.html">
        <NOFRAMES>
                Start with <A HREF="frame4.html">to view this site
                without frames.
        </NOFRAMES>
</FRAMESET>
</HTML>
~
```

Figure 6.2 ■ The source code for Figure 6.1.

page itself does not contain any of your site content at all. Figure 6.1 illustrates a frames page with six windows.

The display presented by Netscape is the result of putting together seven distinct HTML pages, the frame, and six content pages. Each content page can be brought up separately by calling it directly from a URL if one so chooses. Note that the frame windows are filled from left to right, top to bottom. Note, too, the scrollbars in Windows 3 and 5. If a document does not fit in a designated frame window, the scrollbars will appear so that your visitor can move up and down through the document.

The HTML code for Figure 6.1 is shown in Figure 6.2.

Prior to proceeding into the discussion of frames elements and attributes, read through the source code listing. Can you see how the elements function together to produce the Web page in Figure 6.1?

L A B   6 . 2

FRAME ELEMENTS AND ATTRIBUTES

Given the dramatic appearance and functionality of a frames page, there are remarkably few elements and attributes associated with the effect. In fact, there are only three elements.

FRAMESET

FRAMESET defines a frames page. It can in some ways be thought of as a replacement for the BODY element found in a non-frames HTML document. The element delineates the beginning and end of a set of instructions for the browser. Attributes that can be applied to the FRAMESET element include:

> **ROWS**—Sets the height and number of rows in a frameset. Row height can be set as either pixels or percentages of the browser window. In most cases, it is wiser to size your rows using percentages, as a browser will not resize itself automatically to accommodate the number of pixels required to display a frames page. Too many pixels will cause your page to be truncated, and too few will cause the browser to fill the excess space as it sees fit.
>
> **Example:** ROWS="60%,20%,20%" or ROWS="60%,20%,*"
>
> The attribute specifies that the frameset will have three rows with widths of 60%, 20%, and 20% of the browser window. Note that the second example does exactly the same thing—the rows attribute will compute the remaining percentage size for a series of rows if it is not filled in.
>
> **COLS**—Sets the width and number of rows in a frame using either pixels or percentages.
>
> **Example:** COLS="20%,80%" or COLS="20%,*"
>
> Just like ROWS, COLS will compute the percentage value for a remaining column size if necessary.

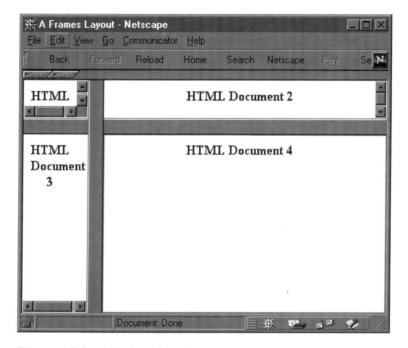

Figure 6.3 ■ A simpler frames page.

FRAMEBORDER—Allows the author to turn frame borders on and off. A value of zero means that no borders should be included.

Example: FRAMEBORDER=0

BORDER—Used to set the width of the frame borders to a certain number of pixels.

Example: BORDER=20

BORDERCOLOR—Used to set the color of frame borders.

Example: BORDERCOLOR=RED or BORDERCOLOR="#ff0000"

Figure 6.3 demonstrates how the appearance of a frames page can change with the addition and modification of the FRAMESOURCE attributes, and Figure 6.4 contains the code for the page. Further, Figure 6.5 displays the same frames page with the FRAMEBORDER attribute set to zero.

FRAME

FRAME contains the content address and attributes for individual FRAMESET windows. Element attributes that function properly in both Netscape and Internet Explorer include:

```
shell3 - SecureCRT
File  Edit  View  Options  Transfer  Script  Window  Help

<HTML>
<HEAD>
<TITLE>A Frames Layout</TITLE>
</HEAD>
<FRAMESET FRAMEBORDER=0 BORDER=20 BORDERCOLOR="#ff0000" ROWS="20%,*" cols="20%,*
">
        <FRAME SRC="frame1.html">
        <FRAME SRC="frame2.html">
        <FRAME SRC="frame3.html">
        <FRAME SRC="frame4.html">
        <NOFRAMES>
                Start with <A HREF="frame4.html">to view this site
                without frames.
        </NOFRAMES>
</FRAMESET>
</HTML>

Ready                        Telnet        11, 9    16 Rows, 80 Cols  VT100
```

Figure 6.4 ■ The source code for Figure 6.3.

SRC—Specifies the URL or filename of the HTML document to be loaded into the window.

Example: <FRAME SRC="frame1.html">

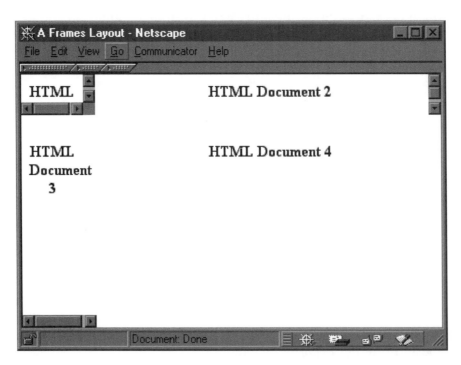

Figure 6.5 ■ A frames document with FRAMEBORDER set to zero.

It is worth mentioning again that a frames document **does not** include any of the content to be displayed in its windows. It is merely a layout for a number of other HTML documents.

NAME—Used to name a window within a frameset so that documents can be loaded to it directly using the TARGET attribute in a link in another window. For instance, referring back to Figure 6.3, if we have a link in Window 3 that wants to display a document's contents in Window 4, the FRAME and HREF code would look something like this:

The frameset: `<FRAME SRC="frame4.html" NAME="four">`

Window 3:   `<A HREF="afile.html" TARGET="four">`

The name of a frameset window can be any text string you like; it does not necessarily need to be a number.

As an aside, TARGET has four standard names that can be used to specify where you would like a linked document to be loaded.

_blank   Loads the document into a newly opened browser window. Be careful with this value, as opening too many browser windows may crash some of your visitors' computers.

_self   Loads the document into the same window as the link. This is the default value for TARGET.

_parent   Loads the document into the parent window or frameset.

_top   Loads the document, removing all frames from the window.

NORESIZE—By default, a user can resize the frame windows in the browser to see more of one particular document or hide another window entirely. The NORESIZE attribute turns off this capability, preserving the integrity of your frames page's appearance and making certain that an end-user does not, for instance, close a window that may have advertising information from a site's sponsor.

Example: `<FRAME SRC=frame4.html" NAME="four" NORESIZE>`

Keep in mind that setting NORESIZE for any window within a frameset will freeze the rest of the windows as well.

SCROLLING—As stated before, scroll bars will appear by default when documents do not fit in the window into which they are loaded. SCROLLING allows the author to state whether or not scroll bars should be displayed regardless of the size of a window's docu-

**LAB
6.2**

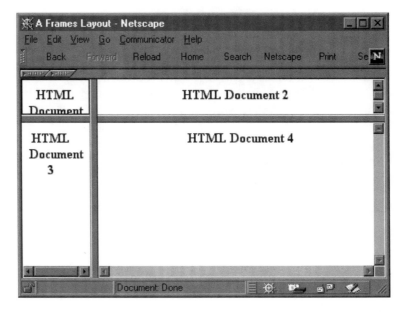

Figure 6.6 ■ **Setting the** `SCROLLING` **attribute.**

ment. `SCROLLING=NO` prevents the display of scroll bars as well as scrolling. `SCROLLING=YES` forces the display of scroll bars even if the entire document fits into a window. Figure 6.6 shows the effects of setting this element for individual windows. Note how scrolling is disabled in Window 1 even though the content document clearly does not fit the window properly. On the other hand, scrollbars appear in Window 4 even though they are not needed. In many cases, it may well be best to let this attribute default.

NOFRAMES AND NO FRAMES

The `NOFRAMES` element is used to enclose a small amount of text, and perhaps a link, to be rendered by browsers that are not able to display frames. Examples of its use can be found in all of the frameset code examples in this chapter. While it is now almost impossible to find current browsers that do not know how to process frames, there are still users out there who have older browsers that do not understand frames or do not render them in an attractive way. Check your frames pages with as many browsers as you possibly can.

When frames first came out, it was not unusual to see something along the lines of, "Your browser doesn't understand frames! Go **here** to download a browser that does!" Imagine the consternation, even irritation, of the hapless visitor that received such a message. Make your `NOFRAMES` content helpful. There is nothing wrong with suggesting a browser that can display your frames site in all its glory, but it is considered to be good form to offer an alternative means of navigating the site without the use of frames.

Also, there are still a number of people who don't care for viewing a site with frames even if they have capable browsers. They may not like looking at more than one page at a time, or it may take their computer too long to download the multiple HTML files it takes to construct a single frames page. Regardless of their reasons, it is a courtesy to offer a link to a non-frames version of your site.

LAB 6.2 EXERCISES

6.2.1   *FRAME ELEMENTS AND ATTRIBUTES*

a) Review the following frameset code, a very popular layout, and think about how the page would be rendered by a browser. Make a rough drawing of how you think the page would look.

```
<HTML>
<HEAD>
<TITLE>A Frames Layout</TITLE>
</HEAD>
<FRAMESET BORDER=10 COLS="20%,*">
        <FRAME SRC="frame1.html" NAME=CONTENTS>
        <FRAME SRC="frame2.html">
        <NOFRAMES>
          Start with <A HREF="frame1.html">
          to view this site without frames.
        </NOFRAMES>
</FRAMESET>
</HTML>
```

b) Produce the HTML code for the following frames page.

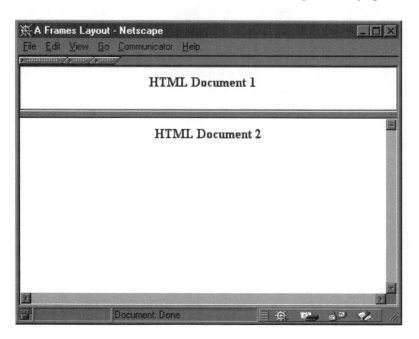

LAB 6.2 EXERCISE ANSWERS

6.2.1 ANSWERS

a) Review the following frameset code, a very popular layout, and think about how the page would be rendered by a browser. Make a rough drawing of how you think the page would look.

Answer: The code on page 151 is rendered as follows by Netscape:

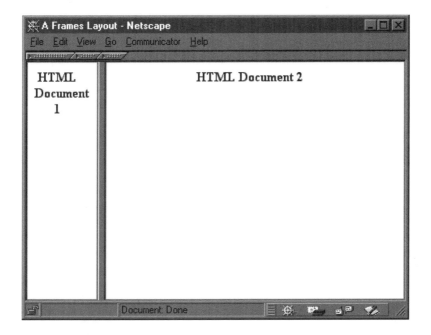

b) Produce the HTML code for the following frames page.

Answer: The source code is:

```
<HTML>
<HEAD>
<TITLE>A Frames Layout</TITLE>
</HEAD>
<FRAMESET BORDER=10 ROWS="20%,*">
        <FRAME SRC="frame1.html" NAME=CONTENTS>
        <FRAME SRC="frame2.html" SCROLLING=YES>
        <NOFRAMES>
            Start with <A HREF="frame1.html">
            to view this site without frames.
        </NOFRAMES>
</FRAMESET>
</HTML>
```

LAB 6.2 SELF-REVIEW QUESTIONS

1)   A Web page should contain as many frames as possible so as to present the user with as much information as possible.
   a) True
   b) False

2)   All browsers understand frames.
   a) True
   b) False

3)   The NOFRAMES element automatically presents a Web page in a non-frames format.
   a) True
   b) False

4)   It is preferable to size frame rows and columns using
   a) Percentages
   b) Pixels

5)   A properly coded frameset rendering four frame windows will involve the use of how many HTML files?
   a) 1
   b) 4
   c) 5

6)   Scroll bars will appear in frame windows by default whether or not a document fits in a given window in its entirety.
   a) True
   b) False

7)   NORESIZE
   a) Prevents the visitor from resizing the browser window
   b) Prevents the visitor from resizing the frame windows
   c) Both of the above

Quiz answers appear in the Appendix, Section 6.2.

L A B   6 . 3

NESTED FRAMES

Consider the frames page in Figure 6.7 and think about how the code for such a page might look. Up until now, we have worked with only one frameset at a time. Figure 6.7 is an example of nested frames—the occurrence of framesets within framesets.

While the call for nested frames is not frequent, it is good to understand how they work.

The code for the frameset is shown in Figure 6.8.

The best way to see what is going on in nested frameset source code is to pull it apart into its separate pieces. In this example, we are working with two sets of frames. The first is defined as two rows, the top one taking up 30% of the browser window and the second filling the balance (see Figure 6.9). The second is a set of three equally sized columns (see Figure 6.10).

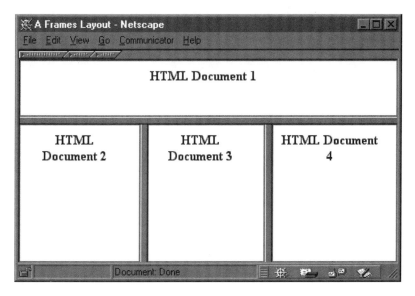

Figure 6.7 ■ Nested frames.

```
shell3 - SecureCRT
File  Edit  View  Options  Transfer  Script  Window  Help

<HTML>
<HEAD>
<TITLE>A Frames Layout</TITLE>
</HEAD>
<FRAMESET ROWS="30%,*" BORDER=10>
        <FRAME SRC="frame1.html" NAME=FRAME1>
        <FRAMESET BORDER=10 COLS="*,*,*">
                <FRAME SRC="frame2.html" NAME=FRAME2>
                <FRAME SRC="frame3.html" NAME=FRAME3>
                <FRAME SRC="frame4.html" NAME=FRAME4>
        </FRAMESET>
        <NOFRAMES>
                Start with <A HREF="frame1.html">to view this site
                without frames.
        </NOFRAMES>
</FRAMESET>
</HTML>
~
Ready                          Telnet      1, 23   18 Rows, 80 Cols  VT100
```

Figure 6.8 ■ The source code for Figure 6.7.

`Frame1.html` is loaded into the first row. Then, instead of loading `frame2.html` into Row 2, as was done for Figure 6.9, a second frameset of three columns is loaded. The second frameset is then closed, `NOFRAMES` text is included, and the first frameset is closed. That's the nest. The trick is to break a complicated idea for a frames page into its parts, thinking in terms of what rows or columns are going to be replaced by additional framesets.

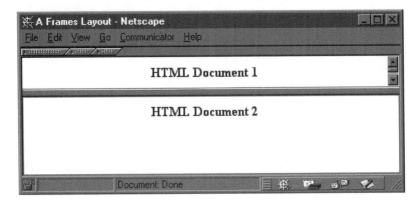

Figure 6.9 ■ Frameset 1 of Figure 6.7.

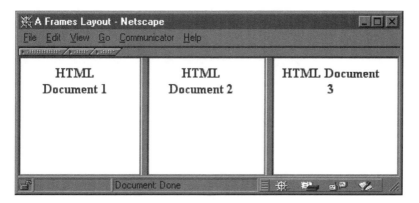

Figure 6.10 ■ Frameset 2 of Figure 6.7.

LAB 6.3 EXERCISE

6.3.1 NESTED FRAMES

While you're not likely to ever want a frames page with so many windows, modify the code for Figure 6.7 so that your final result looks like this:

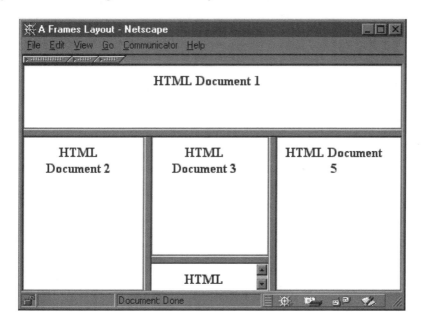

LAB 6.3 EXERCISE ANSWER

6.3.1 ANSWER

While you're not likely to ever want a frames page with so many windows, modify the code for Figure 6.7 so that your final result looks like this:

Answer:

```
shell3 - SecureCRT                                    _ □ ×
File  Edit  View  Options  Transfer  Script  Window  Help

<HTML>
<HEAD>
<TITLE>A Frames Layout</TITLE>
</HEAD>
<FRAMESET ROWS="30%,*" BORDER=10>
        <FRAME SRC="frame1.html" NAME=FRAME1>
        <FRAMESET BORDER=10 COLS="*,*,*">
                <FRAME SRC="frame2.html" NAME=FRAME2>
                <FRAMESET BORDER=10 ROWS="80%,*">
                        <FRAME SRC="frame3.html" NAME=FRAME3>
                        <FRAME SRC="frame4.html" NAME=FRAME4>
                </FRAMESET>
                <FRAME SRC="frame5.html" NAME=FRAME5>
        </FRAMESET>
        <NOFRAMES>
                Start with <A HREF="frame1.html">to view this site
                without frames.
        </NOFRAMES>
</FRAMESET>
</HTML>
~
~

Ready                        Telnet      1, 16   22 Rows, 80 Cols  VT100
```

LAB 6.3 SELF-REVIEW QUESTION

1) Nested frames are best thought of as
   a) A frameset with many windows
   b) A frameset within a frameset
   c) A frame that contains two HTML files

Quiz answer appears in the Appendix, Section 6.3.

L A B 6 . 4

A QUICK WORD ABOUT INLINE FRAMES

Internet Explorer supports inline frames, a nice feature that allows you to include a small frameset within an otherwise non-frames document. Any other browser does not, to date, support them, but it is still worthwhile to take a look at them. Figure 6.11 is an example of inline frames as rendered by IE. Figure 6.12 shows the same page rendered by Netscape, provided appropriate text is included in the HTML.

The concept in this example is that a user can click on one of the words in the left-hand window and a definition will appear on the right. For instance, if the user selects Pomegranate, the effect would be a window such as that shown in Figure 6.13.

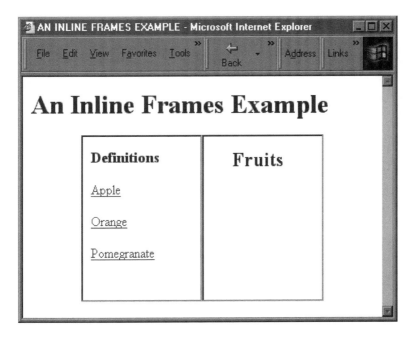

Figure 6.11 ■ An inline frameset as rendered by Internet Explorer.

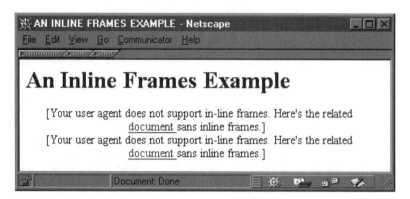

Figure 6.12 ■ Inline frames as rendered by Netscape.

Inline frames involve only one element and a few attributes. IFRAME opens a window of a size defined in pixels by the HEIGHT and WIDTH attributes. NAME is used exactly as it is with the FRAME element. It names a particular window so that it can be the target of a link from another window. FRAMEBORDER is used to set the width of the borders in pixels.

The ALIGN attribute, which is not used in this example, is used to align the inline frames with the rest of the text on a page. As with images and tables, the accepted values for ALIGN are TOP, MIDDLE, BOTTOM, LEFT, and RIGHT, and the effects of the attribute are the same.

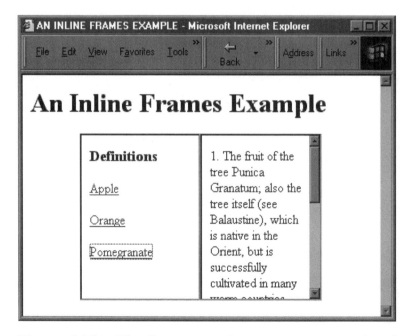

Figure 6.13 ■ The frameset after Pomegranate is selected.

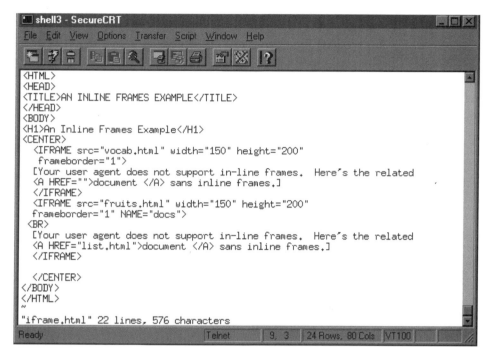

```
<HTML>
<HEAD>
<TITLE>AN INLINE FRAMES EXAMPLE</TITLE>
</HEAD>
<BODY>
<H1>An Inline Frames Example</H1>
<CENTER>
  <IFRAME src="vocab.html" width="150" height="200"
   frameborder="1">
  [Your user agent does not support in-line frames.  Here's the related
  <A HREF="">document </A> sans inline frames.]
  </IFRAME>
  <IFRAME src="fruits.html" width="150" height="200"
  frameborder="1" NAME="docs">
  <BR>
  [Your user agent does not support in-line frames.  Here's the related
  <A HREF="list.html">document </A> sans inline frames.]
  </IFRAME>

  </CENTER>
</BODY>
</HTML>
~
"iframe.html" 22 lines, 576 characters
```

Figure 6.14 ■ **The source code for Figure 6.11.**

The full source code for the inline frames example here is shown in Figure 6.14.

CHAPTER 6

TEST YOUR THINKING

The projects in this section use the skills you've acquired in this chapter. The answers to these projects are available to instructors only through a Prentice Hall sales representative and are intended to be used in classroom discussion and assessment.

By now you should have a good handle on the functionality and coding of frames. You should also have a fair idea as to whether or not they are a style that you want to use on your Web site. Even if you have decided that they are not to your liking, it is to your benefit to be able to produce frames pages. Someone is bound to ask for them.

1) Create a Web page that contains two frames; the left is a list of clickable links to pages whose content will be displayed in the right frame.

2) Provide your visitors with the option of navigating your site without frames and make sure the proper navigation links appear on all of the pages you created in exercise 1.

CHAPTER 7

FORMS

  Form ever follows function.

Louis Henri Sullivan
"The Tall Office Building Artistically Considered" (1896)

CHAPTER OBJECTIVES

In this chapter, you will learn about:

✔ When to use a form	Page 164
✔ Form elements	Page 165
✔ How to collect form information	Page 177
✔ Using tables to format forms	Page 178

Forms add a level of interactivity to your Web site that goes beyond that of hyperactive and mailto links. Visitors provide requested information on a form with the expectation of receiving something in return, be it merchandise, information, or simply a response. The form is a vehicle for true give-and-take activity between a Web site visitor and the site owner.

L A B 7 . 1

WHEN TO USE A FORM

While mailto elements, discussed in Chapter 3, allow a site visitor to send email from a Web page to another individual, they are limited. Essentially, all they do is open the browser's email program and fill in the To: field with a specific address. Your visitor then enters whatever they please and sends the message. What if, though, you need to collect very specific information from your visitor to follow through completely?

This is where forms come in. Forms allow you to collect the information you need via a system of elements that include limited-length fields, free-form text areas, pull-down selection menus, buttons, and multiple choice checkboxes. You can even process forms with programs that will require indicated fields to be completed with appropriate information before the visitor can continue.

Forms, as useful as they are, are no more difficult to master than any other set of HTML elements. In fact, the most difficult part of a form is deciding on the information it needs to solicit.

L A B   7 . 2

FORM ELEMENTS

The following is the code for a simple form. Figure 7.1 illustrates how Netscape renders the form. Note that you can, and should, include other HTML elements such as images and text in your form.

```
<HTML>
<HEAD>
<TITLE>A Simple Form</TITLE>
</HEAD>
<BODY BGCOLOR="ffffff" TEXT="darkgreen">
<FORM METHOD=POST ACTION="mailto:arlyn@shore.net">
<H2>A Simple Form</H2>
Please complete the following form and submit it when
complete.
All information will be kept strictly confidential.
Thank you.
<BR><BR>
<!-- Text Fields -->
<B>First Name: </B><INPUT TYPE=TEXT NAME=FNAME
SIZE=20 MAXLENGTH=30>
<B>Last Name: </B><INPUT TYPE=TEXT NAME=LNAME SIZE=20
MAXLENGTH=30><BR>
<BR>
<!-- Radio Buttons -->
<B>Sex: </B><INPUT TYPE=RADIO NAME=SEX VALUE="Male">
Male
<INPUT TYPE=RADIO NAME=SEX VALUE="Female"> Female
<BR><BR>
<!-- Scrolling Menu -->
<B>I live in the: </B>
     <SELECT NAME=REGION SIZE=2>
<OPTION VALUE=NE>Northeast
<OPTION VALUE=MA>Middle Atlantic
<OPTION VALUE=SE>Southeast
<OPTION VALUE=MW>Midwest
<OPTION VALUE=NW>Northwest
<OPTION VALUE=W>West
```

```
<OPTION VALUE=SW>Southwest
        </SELECT>
<!--Pull-down Menu -->
<B>I would rather live in the: </B>
        <SELECT NAME=WISH>
<OPTION VALUE=NE>Northeast
<OPTION VALUE=MA>Middle Atlantic
<OPTION VALUE=SE>Southeast
<OPTION VALUE=MW>Midwest
<OPTION VALUE=NW>Northwest
<OPTION VALUE=W>West
<OPTION VALUE=SW>Southwest
        </SELECT>
<BR><BR>
<!-- Checkboxes -->
<B>I have been to the following continents: </B>
<BR>
<INPUT TYPE=CHECKBOX NAME=BEENTO VALUE="Europe">Eu-
rope
<INPUT TYPE=CHECKBOX NAME=BEENTO VALUE="Asia">Asia
<INPUT TYPE=CHECKBOX NAME=BEENTO VALUE="South Amer-
ica">South America
<INPUT TYPE=CHECKBOX NAME=BEENTO
VALUE="Australia">Australia
<INPUT TYPE=CHECKBOX NAME=BEENTO
VALUE="Antartica">Antartica
<BR><BR>
<!-- Textarea -->
<B>Why, in 25 words or less, you should send me to
the destination
of my choice: </B>
<BR>
        <TEXTAREA NAME=WHY COLS=50 ROWS=2 WRAP=PHYSICAL>
        </TEXTAREA>
<BR><BR>
<!-- Submit or Clear -->
<INPUT TYPE=SUBMIT> <INPUT TYPE=RESET>
</FORM>
</BODY>
</HTML>
```

Given the experience you have gained in working with HTML elements in the previous chapters, you can probably read through the code for this form and understand what is happening. Still, it is worth spending some time here looking at each element and its attributes in some detail.

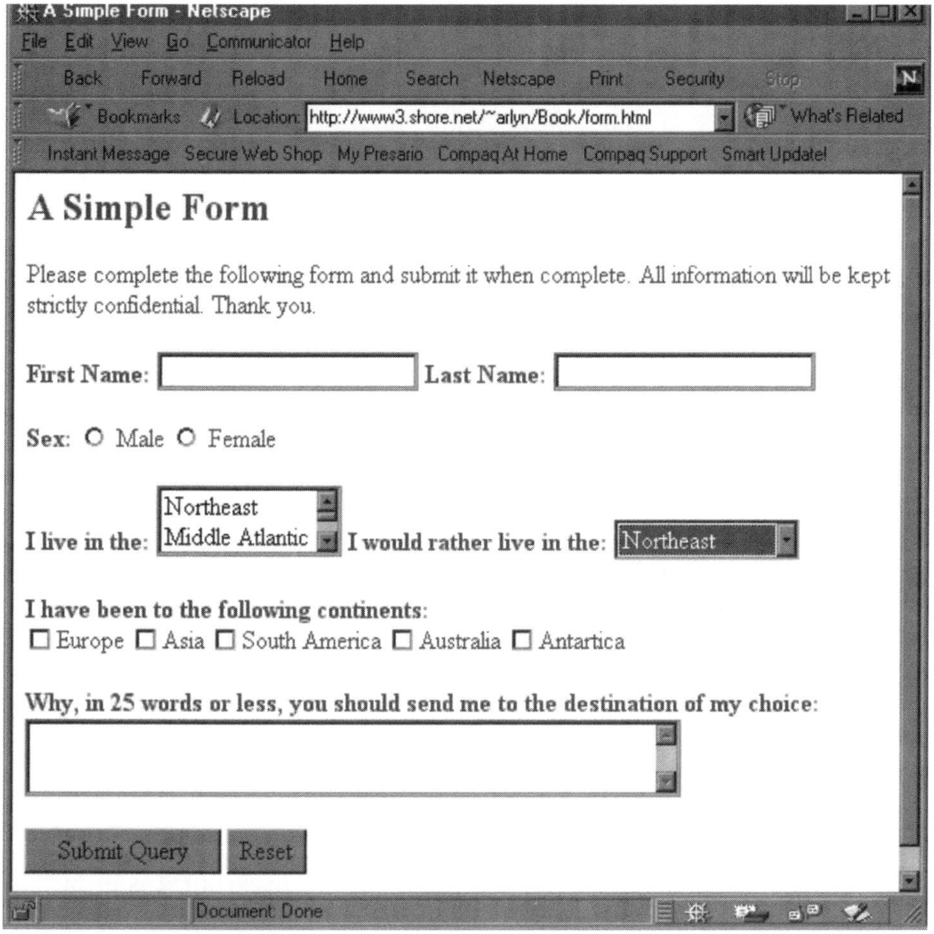

Figure 7.1 ■ A simple form.

FORM

The FORM element surrounds all of the content of your form and takes two attributes, METHOD and ACTION. For our purposes here, it is enough to know that the form will be processed using mailto, the information will be sent to `arlyn@shore.net`, and the method will be POST.

INPUT

An INPUT element takes information typed by the Web page visitor and processes it accordingly. Attributes for the element include:

TYPE   The type of input field to render.

        TYPE=TEXT

Text fields provide a single line of input space in a form.

TYPE=RADIO

Radio buttons are a series of circular buttons used to select one and only one answer (in our example, either Male or Female). If one button is selected, regardless of the number of buttons presented, the remaining buttons are automatically de-selected. The name "radio buttons" is derived from the concept of buttons on a radio—if you push one, you tune in to a single station. It is not possible, under normal circumstances, to listen to two radio stations at once using a single radio.

TYPE=CHECKBOX

A checkbox is used to render a set of choices when the user can select more than one answer. For instance, a visitor to the form in Figure 7.1 is able to select any number of the continents listed and the results of the selection will be processed accordingly.

TYPE=SUBMIT

Submit creates a button on the form that the user can click when they are ready to send the data.

TYPE=RESET

Reset creates a button that allows the user to clear the form entirely.

NAME	The name, or label, of the variable to be processed. This attribute is invisible to the form user, but it is important when the information from the form is passed on. Consider Figure 7.2, which illustrates how the form entries arrive in a mail message. The format isn't pretty but, as you can see, it is entirely possible to determine what information was entered in each form field because of the names, or labels.
SIZE	Specifies the display length of the text field on the form.
MAXLENGTH	Specifies the maximum length of the entry for a field. Note that it is possible for the entry length to be larger than the length of the displayed text field.
VALUE	In the case of radio buttons and checkboxes, this is the actual text submitted for a selected field when the form's Submit button is clicked. VALUE can also be used to set the default text for text fields and the text on your Submit and Reset buttons.

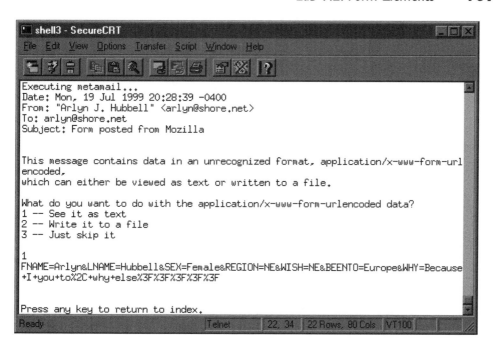

Figure 7.2 ■ Information from a form received by email.

SELECT

The SELECT element is used to construct scrolling and pull-down menus. The element can take on all of the attributes listed above except TYPE, and it is the SIZE attribute that determines the style of menu to be rendered. If the SIZE attribute is set, for instance to 6, a six-line scrolling menu will be generated and the user will be able to scroll up and down to see any additional items. If SIZE is omitted, a pull-down menu will appear with one item in the starting window. When the user clicks the menu button, as much of the rest of the menu as possible will pop up on the screen.

An additional attribute, MULTIPLE, can be used with scrolling menus. This should be used when you want your visitors to be able to select a number of entries from a menu.

OPTION

OPTION defines the items included in select menus. The value of OPTION can be set using the VALUE attribute or it can be left to default to the content of the element itself. For example, in Figure 7.1, if the value of the first option in the pull-down menu were not set to "NE," it would default to "Northeast."

There are more attributes uniquely associated with the OPTION element.

LABEL Another means of displaying the contents of a menu item. To illustrate, the following two lines of code produce identical menu entries:

```
<OPTION LABEL=Antartica>
```

```
<OPTION>Antartica
```

SELECTED Labels the option you wish to be selected and submitted if no other item is chosen.

TEXTAREA

Windows for the entry of free-form text are created using the TEXTAREA element. This is where your visitor might enter additional comments that weren't prompted by any other questions, or perhaps cut and paste requested material from another document. By including text (and text only, no elements) between <TEXTAREA> and </TEXTAREA>, you are also able to provide a simple template for data entry which your visitor can modify if you allow it. Two attributes are associated with TEXTAREA:

ROWS Sets the height of a textarea to a number of rows.

COLS Sets the width of a textarea to a number of columns.

FUTURE ELEMENTS

Finally, the HTML 4.0 standard calls for a number of new elements that are not yet recognized by current browsers. The LABEL element will allow the user to build sophisticated labels for multiple fields. FIELDSET and LEGEND provide the ability to group form elements into labeled, specially displayed sections. And, form users will be able to move between defined sections of a form using the ACCESSKEY attribute, which will allow the author to assign "hot keys" as navigation tools.

LAB 7.2 EXERCISES

7.2.1 FORM ELEMENTS

a) You are taking a survey regarding people's color preferences and have a list of seven you would like them to choose from: red, orange, yellow, green, blue, indigo, and violet.

> **1)** Write two blocks of HTML that will allow the user to select only one color.

_____

_____

> **2)** Write two blocks of HTML that will allow the user to select as many colors as they please.

_____

_____

b) Reproduce the following form:

LAB 7.2 EXERCISE ANSWERS

7.2.1 ANSWERS

a) You are taking a survey regarding people's color preferences and have a list of seven you would like them to choose from: red, orange, yellow, green, blue, indigo, and violet.

  1) Write two blocks of HTML that will allow the user to select only one color.

  Answer: `<FORM METHOD=POST ACTION="mailto:arlyn@shore.net" >`
  `<P>`
  `Please select your preferred color:<BR>`
  `<SELECT NAME=COLOR>`

```
<OPTION VALUE=Red LABEL=Red>
<OPTION VALUE=Ora LABEL=Orange>
<OPTION VALUE=Yel LABEL=Yellow>
<OPTION VALUE=Gre LABEL=Green>
      <OPTION VALUE=Blu LABEL=Blue>
      <OPTION VALUE=Ind LABEL=Indigo>
      <OPTION VALUE=Vio LABEL=Violet>
</SELECT>
<INPUT TYPE=SUBMIT>
</FORM>
```

**LAB
7.2**

or:

```
<FORM METHOD=POST ACTION="mailto:arlyn@shore.net">
<P>
Please select your preferred color:<BR>
<INPUT TYPE=RADIO NAME=COLOR VALUE="red">Red
<INPUT TYPE=RADIO NAME=COLOR VALUE="ora">Orange
<INPUT TYPE=RADIO NAME=COLOR VALUE="yel">Yellow
<INPUT TYPE=RADIO NAME=COLOR VALUE="gre">Green
<INPUT TYPE=RADIO NAME=COLOR VALUE="blu">Blue
<INPUT TYPE=RADIO NAME=COLOR VALUE="ind">Indigo
<INPUT TYPE=RADIO NAME=COLOR VALUE="vio">Violet
<BR><BR>
<INPUT TYPE=SUBMIT>
</FORM>
```

2) Write two blocks of HTML that will allow the user to select as many colors as they please.

Answer:
```
<FORM METHOD=POST ACTION="mailto:arlyn@ shore.net">
<P>
Please select your preferred color:<BR>
<SELECT NAME=COLOR SIZE=3 MULTIPLE>
<OPTION VALUE=Red LABEL=Red>
<OPTION VALUE=Ora LABEL=Orange>
<OPTION VALUE=Yel LABEL=Yellow>
<OPTION VALUE=Gre LABEL=Green>
      <OPTION VALUE=Blu LABEL=Blue>
      <OPTION VALUE=Ind LABEL=Indigo>
      <OPTION VALUE=Vio LABEL=Violet>
</SELECT>
<INPUT TYPE=SUBMIT>
</FORM>
```

or:

```
<FORM METHOD=POST ACTION="mailto:arlyn@shore.net">
<P>
Please select your preferred color:<BR>
<INPUT TYPE=CHECKBOX NAME=COLOR VALUE="red">Red
<INPUT TYPE=CHECKBOX NAME=COLOR VALUE="ora">
Orange
<INPUT TYPE=CHECKBOX NAME=COLOR VALUE="yel">
Yellow
<INPUT TYPE=CHECKBOX NAME=COLOR VALUE="gre">Green
<INPUT TYPE=CHECKBOX NAME=COLOR VALUE="blu">Blue
<INPUT TYPE=CHECKBOX NAME=COLOR VALUE="ind">
Indigo
<INPUT TYPE=CHECKBOX NAME=COLOR VALUE="vio">
Violet
<BR><BR>
<INPUT TYPE=SUBMIT>
</FORM>
```

b) Reproduce the following form:

Answer:
```
<HTML>
<HEAD>
<TITLE>A Form Exercise</TITLE>
</HEAD>
<BODY BGCOLOR="ffffff" TEXT="darkgreen">
<FORM METHOD=POST ACTION="mailto:arlyn@shore.net">
<H2>A Form Exercise</H2>
Please complete the following form and submit it
when complete.
All information will be kept strictly confidential.
Thank you.
<BR><BR>
<B><I>First Name: </I></B><INPUT TYPE=TEXT
NAME=FNAME SIZE=20 MAXLENGTH=30><BR>
<B><I>Last Name: </I></B><INPUT TYPE=TEXT
NAME=LNAME SIZE=20 MAXLENGTH=30><BR>
<BR>
<B><I>Street Address: </I></B><INPUT TYPE=TEXT
NAME=ADD SIZE=20 MAXLENGTH=30><BR>
<B><I>Apt. Number: </I></B><INPUT TYPE=TEXT
NAME=APT SIZE=20 MAXLENGTH=30><BR>
<B><I>City: </I></B><INPUT TYPE=TEXT NAME=CITY
SIZE=20 MAXLENGTH=30><BR>
<B><I>State: </I></B><INPUT TYPE=TEXT NAME=STATE
SIZE=2 MAXLENGTH=2>
```

```
<B><I>Zip Code: </I></B><INPUT TYPE=TEXT NAME=ZIP
SIZE=10 MAXLENGTH=10><BR>
<BR><BR>
<B><I>I intend to relocate in the next 12 months:
</I></B>
        <INPUT TYPE=RADIO NAME=RELO VALUE="Y">
Yes
        <INPUT TYPE=RADIO NAME=RELO VALUE="N"> No
        <INPUT TYPE=RADIO NAME=RELO
VALUE="NS">Not Sure
<BR><BR>
<B><I>Please send me information on the following
regions: </I></B>
        <SELECT NAME=REGION SIZE=4 MULTIPLE>
            <OPTION VALUE=NE>Northeast
            <OPTION VALUE=MA>Middle Atlantic
            <OPTION VALUE=SE>Southeast
            <OPTION VALUE=MW>Midwest
            <OPTION VALUE=NW>Northwest
            <OPTION VALUE=W>West
            <OPTION VALUE=SW>Southwest
        </SELECT>
<BR><BR>
<B><I>The following things are important to me:
</I></B>
<BR>
    <INPUT TYPE=CHECKBOX NAME=IMP
VALUE="Food">Fine Restaurants
    <INPUT TYPE=CHECKBOX NAME=IMP
VALUE="Cine">Theatre and Film
    <INPUT TYPE=CHECKBOX NAME=IMP
VALUE="LocPol">Local Politics
<INPUT TYPE=CHECKBOX NAME=IMP VALUE="Nite">Night
Life
    <INPUT TYPE=CHECKBOX NAME=IMP
VALUE="Nat">Getting Back to Nature
    <INPUT TYPE=CHECKBOX NAME=IMP
VALUE="Sol">Solitude
<BR><BR>
<INPUT TYPE=SUBMIT> <INPUT TYPE=RESET>
</FORM>
</BODY>
</HTML>
```

**LAB
7.2**

LAB 7.2 SELF-REVIEW QUESTIONS

1) Radio buttons allow
   a) Multiple selections
   b) Only one selection

2) SIZE specifies the maximum length of a text field entry.
   a) True
   b) False

3) VALUE is used to
   a) Assign the text submitted when radio buttons and checkboxes are selected
   b) Assign the default value for text fields
   c) Assign text on Submit and Reset buttons
   d) All of the above

4) Checkboxes allow
   a) Multiple selections
   b) Only one selection

5) COLS and ROWS are used to
   a) Limit the amount of information entered in a textarea
   b) Size a textarea window
   c) Both of the above

6) SELECT is used to create
   a) Scrolling menus
   b) Pull-down menus
   c) Both of the above

7) SIZE, when used in conjunction with SELECT, creates a
   a) Scrolling menu
   b) Pull-down menu
   c) Both of the above

   Quiz answers appear in the Appendix, Section 7.2.

L A B   7 . 3

COLLECTING FORM INFORMATION

How you collect data from your forms is a matter of preference and the technical tools available to you. The point is to choose a method that will be comfortable and efficient for both you and your clients.

As we saw in the form at the beginning of this chapter, it is possible to use mailto to transmit form field names and entered information via email. The output is not formatted for ease of use, but it is readable and other programs can be used to parse the data into a more usable format.

Other programs and scripts are available as well, many of them free on the Web and some which are very sophisticated. Features you will find in many of these programs include confirmation pages after a form is sent, more readable delivery of data, and the ability to require some or all fields in a form. To use these programs, you will need cgi bin privileges for your Web site. Check with your ISP to verify your privileges and what types of scripts they will permit on their public servers. You may even find that they have form scripts available for your use.

Depending on what sort of information you are soliciting with your form, you may need to look into methods of encrypting data while it is in transit over the Web. It may also be necessary to encrypt any files you are using to store data received from your forms.

Finally, it is worth mentioning that Web transmission is not the only way of collecting the information that people provide through your forms. It is not unusual to see forms on the Web that need to be printed out and either faxed or mailed to the recipient.

Again, it is all a matter of preference and the resources you have at hand.

L A B   7 . 4

USING TABLES TO FORMAT FORMS

As you probably noticed while looking at the form in Figure 7.1 and creating the form required in the last exercise, forms do not lend themselves to any sort of sophisticated formatting. This is especially apparent in the form you wrote in the exercise. You can see that, while all of the required fields can be coded into a page, the end result is not as easy to read as it might be, nor is it terribly pleasing to the eye.

While present HTML standards dictate the use of style sheets to format forms, many Web site designers prefer to use tables as a workaround for this particular dilemma. The coding can be tedious, but the end results can be worth it and are more universally compatible at this point in time. Especially with very long forms, the use of tables to organize the fields can make the difference between a user taking the time to complete the form or giving up because it is impossible to follow.

Figure 7.3 shows a simple form that is very short, but rather messy in appearance. Take a minute to think about what the HTML code for the form might be. Now think about how you might use the table elements you learned in Chapter 5 to rearrange the form into a more organized format. Figure 7.4 illustrates one way of doing it, and the HTML code is as follows:

```
<HTML>
<HEAD>
<TITLE>A Form Using Tables</TITLE>
</HEAD>
<BODY BGCOLOR="ffffff" TEXT="darkgreen">
<FORM METHOD=POST ACTION="mailto:arlyn@shore.net">
<H2>We Need Your Contact Information</H2>
We are collecting contact information for a new com-
pany directory.
All information is for internal use only and will be
kept strictly
```

```
confidential.
Thank you.
<BR><BR>
<TABLE>
<TR>
<TD><B>First Name: </B></TD>
<TD><INPUT TYPE=TEXT NAME=FNAME SIZE=12
MAXLENGTH=20></TD>
<TD><B>Last Name: </B></TD>
<TD><INPUT TYPE=TEXT NAME=LNAME SIZE=12
MAXLENGTH=20></TD>
</TR>
<TR><TD><BR></TD></TR>
<TR>
<TD><B>Phone Numbers:</B></TD>
</TR>
<TR>
<TD><B>Office: </B></TD>
<TD><INPUT TYPE=TEXT NAME=OFF SIZE=10
MAXLENGTH=10></TD>
<TD><B>Home: </B></TD>
<TD><INPUT TYPE=TEXT NAME=HOM SIZE=10
MAXLENGTH=10></TD>
</TR>
<TR>
<TD><B>Cell: </B></TD>
<TD><INPUT TYPE=TEXT NAME=CEL SIZE=10
MAXLENGTH=10></TD>
<TD><B>Pager: </B></TD>
<TD><INPUT TYPE=TEXT NAME=PAG1 SIZE=10
MAXLENGTH=10></TD>
</TR>
<TR><TD><BR></TD></TR>
<TR>
<TD COLSPAN=4>
<B>Email Addresses:</B>
</TD>
</TR>
<TR>
<TD><B>Pager: </B></TD>
<TD><INPUT TYPE=TEXT NAME=PAG2 SIZE=20
MAXLENGTH=30></TD>
<TD><B>Personal: </B></TD>
<TD><INPUT TYPE=TEXT NAME=EMAIL SIZE=20
MAXLENGTH=30></TD>
```

```
</TR>
<TR><TD><BR></TD></TR>
<TR>
<TD VALIGN=TOP>
<B>I prefer to be: </B>
</TD>
<TD>
            <INPUT TYPE=RADIO NAME=PREF VALUE="Page">
Paged First<BR>
            <INPUT TYPE=RADIO NAME=PREF VALUE="N">
Phoned First
</TD>
</TR>
<TR><TD><BR></TD></TR>
<TR>
<TD COLSPAN=4>
<B>Indicate the holidays during which you will be
available this year: </B>
</TD>
</TR>
<TR>
        <TD><INPUT TYPE=CHECKBOX NAME=AVAIL
VALUE="1">New Year's</TD>
        <TD><INPUT TYPE=CHECKBOX NAME=AVAIL
VALUE="2">Presidents' Day</TD>
        <TD><INPUT TYPE=CHECKBOX NAME=AVAIL
VALUE="3">MLK Day</TD>
</TR>
<TR>
        <TD><INPUT TYPE=CHECKBOX NAME=AVAIL
VALUE="4">Easter</TD>
<TD><INPUT TYPE=CHECKBOX NAME=AVAIL VALUE="5">
Memorial Day</TD>
        <TD><INPUT TYPE=CHECKBOX NAME=AVAIL
VALUE="6">July 4th</TD>
</TR>
<TR>
        <TD><INPUT TYPE=CHECKBOX NAME=AVAIL
VALUE="7">Labor Day</TD>
        <TD><INPUT TYPE=CHECKBOX NAME=AVAIL
VALUE="8">Thanksgiving</TD>
        <TD><INPUT TYPE=CHECKBOX NAME=AVAIL
VALUE="9">Christmas</TD>
</TR>
<TR><TD><BR><BR></TD></TR>
```

```
<TR>
<TD><INPUT TYPE=SUBMIT></TD> <TD><INPUT
TYPE=RESET></TD>
</TR>
</TABLE>
</FORM>
</BODY>
</HTML>
```

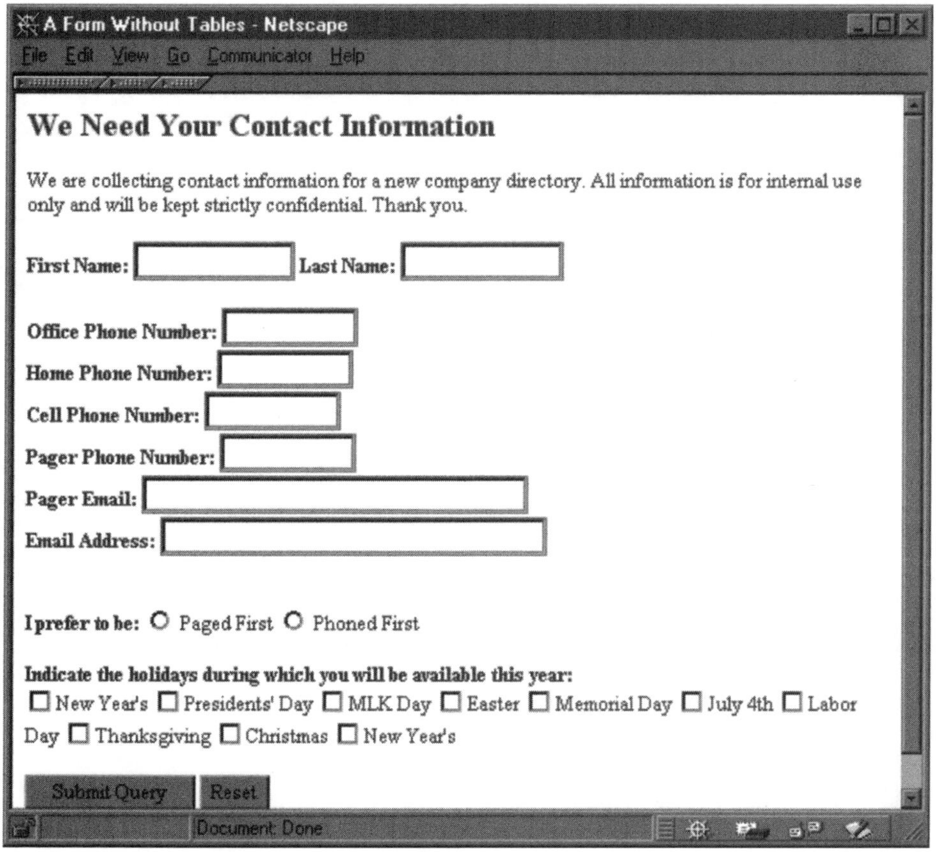

Figure 7.3 ■ A form to be tabled.

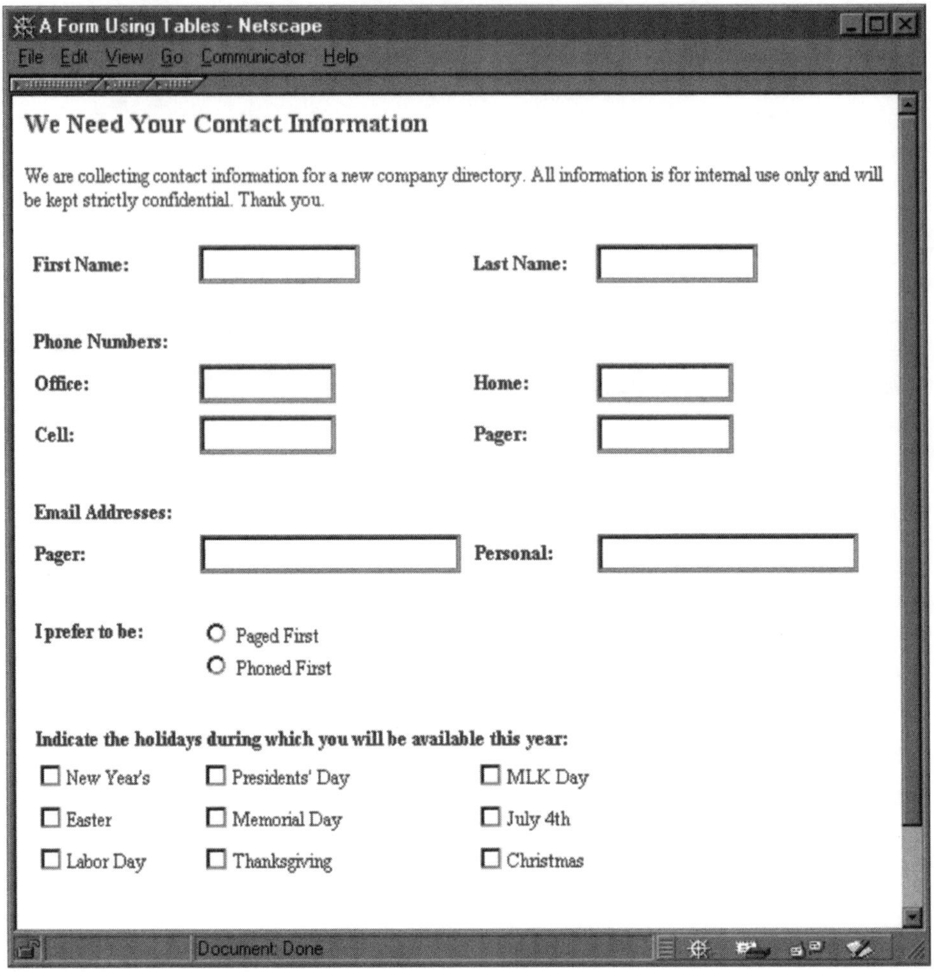

Figure 7.4 ■ The form tabled.

LAB 7.4 EXERCISE

7.4.1 USING TABLES TO FORMAT FORMS

Return to the form you created in Exercise 7.1 and use tables to reformat it so that it will be more aesthetically pleasing and easier to read.

C H A P T E R 7

TEST YOUR THINKING

The projects in this section use the skills you've acquired in this chaper. The answers to these projects are available to instructors only through a Prentice Hall sales representative and are intended to be used in classroom discussion and assessment.

Develop and code a form that can be used to solicit information from visitors to your Web site. Format the page using tables, and use the following elements:

1) A set of radio buttons allowing the visitor to select only one publication on a monthly basis.

2) Text field where the visitor's name, street address, and email address will be entered.

3) Select and include an element that will allow the visitor to tell you how he or she wishes to receive the publication: by email, postal mail, or both.

C H A P T E R   8

SERVER SIDE INCLUDES

 We have had a jolly good lesson, and it serves us jolly well right!

Rudyard Kipling
The Lesson (1901)

CHAPTER OBJECTIVES

In this chapter, you will learn about:

Up until now, everything you wanted to appear on a Web page had to exist physically in the HTML file that generated the page. With the use of Server Side Includes (SSIs), that all changes.

L A B   8 . 1

HOW SERVER SIDE INCLUDES WORK

Server Side Includes, or SSIs as they are often called, are part of a process by which server information is pulled into an HTML file for display. They are popular as they provide the HTML author with the ability to display "live" information, such as the time and date, and execute UNIX commands with the output directed to the Web page.

Server Side Includes are also extremely useful when incorporating the content of a single file in multiple HTML documents. This strategy saves time and improves the uniformity and accuracy of Web pages in that information that is displayed by many pages can be maintained in one file with updates applied site-wide.

The downside to all this is that SSIs require additional processing by the server, which in turn draws on the system resources of the machine hosting your Web site. While any one command may seem trivial on its own, large numbers of requests for SSI processing at any one time may cause a host machine to visibly lag for all users, not just those who are viewing your pages. For this reason, some ISPs choose not to enable SSIs on their servers.

Server Side Includes are a default feature of Apache, the Web server we recommend. They are also available on NCSA and Netscape. CERN, the original Web server and no longer as prevalent as it once was, can process SSIs only if a Perl program called `fakessi` is installed. If you are uncertain as to which Web server you're working with or whether you are able to use SSIs, check with your ISP or system administrator.

Up to this point, it has been standard procedure to name HTML files with an extension of either `.htm` or `.html`. When a file requires SSI processing, that extension will often need to be changed according to your system's requirements. The server that hosts the example files for this chapter requires an extension of `.shtml` for those HTML files needing SSI

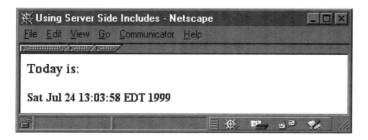

Figure 8.1 ■ Using SSIs to display the date and time.

processing. In this way, Apache knows to look for SSI instructions, or directives, in a file and will handle them appropriately.

Figure 8.1 illustrates the use of SSIs to display the current time and date on a Web page. The actual time and date are produced by executing the UNIX DATE command from the Web page itself.

The "include" nature of SSI directives can best be seen by comparing the source of an .shtml file with the code that is displayed when a page is looked at with a browser's "View Source" facility. Examine the source code presented in Figures 8.2 and 8.3.

Note how the line `<!--#exec cmd="date"-->` in Figure 8.2 is replaced with the current time and date in Figure 8.3. This is the include. Apache has read the directive in the original HTML, retrieved the requested server information, and has inserted it back into the HTML for the browser to display. Note that the original .shtml file on the server is not physically modified in any way.

Figure 8.2 ■ The .shtml source code for Figure 8.1.

```
Source of: http://www3.shore.net/~arlyn/Book/Example...

<HTML>
<HEAD>
<TITLE>Using Server Side Includes</TITLE>
</HEAD>
<BODY BGCOLOR="#ffffff">
<H3>Today is:</H3>
<B>
Sat Jul 24 13:13:53 EDT 1999

</B>
</BODY>
</HTML>
```

Figure 8.3 ■ The source code for Figure 8.1 using View Source.

The value of displaying the date and time using Server Side Includes is that the information displayed will always be current. Each time the page is refreshed, the time and date will be updated. The page can now be called **dynamic.**

The four SSI directives that will be addressed in this chapter are:

echo   Displays environment variables.

include Pulls content from an external file into the .shtml file containing the directive.

exec   Executes a command or CGI program.

config   Formats SSI output.

LAB 8.1   EXERCISES

8.1.1   HOW SERVER SIDE INCLUDES WORK

a) What is the purpose of using Server Side Includes?

_____

_____

b) Which Web servers offer Server Side Includes processing by default?

_____

_____

c) How does a Web server know to process a file for Server Side Includes?

_____

_____

d) What directive would you use in each of the following circumstances?

  1) Execute a CGI script.

_____

_____

  2) Format the output of an SSI directive.

_____

_____

  3) Execute a UNIX command.

_____

_____

  4) Include the content of an external file.

_____

_____

LAB 8.1 EXERCISE ANSWERS

8.1.1 ANSWERS

a)   What is the purpose of using Server Side Includes?

Answer: Server Side Includes allow external information to be included in an HTML file.

b)   Which Web servers offer Server Side Includes processing by default?

Answer: Apache, NCSA, and Netscape.

c)   How does a Web server know to process a file for Server Side Includes?

*Answer: The server, unless it processes **all** files for SSIs, looks for a special filename extension such as* .shtml.

d)   What directive would you use in each of the following circumstances?

   1)   Execute a CGI script.

   Answer: exec

   2)   Format the output of an SSI directive.

   Answer: config

   3)   Execute a UNIX command.

   Answer: exec

   4)   Include the content of an external file.

   Answer: include

LAB 8.1 SELF-REVIEW QUESTIONS

1)   The processing of Server Side Includes is done by the
   a)   Web browser
   b)   Host machine
   c)   User's desktop machine

2)   All ISPs offer Server Side Includes capability.
   a)   True
   b)   False

3) If one views the source of a Web page using Server Side Includes, they will see
   a) The Server Side Includes code
   b) The results of Server Side Includes processing
   c) Both of the above

4) Server Side Includes can be used to
   a) Process and display current system information
   b) Execute commands
   c) Load external files into the current HTML document
   d) All of the above

Quiz answers appear in the Appendix, Section 8.1.

L A B 8 . 2

INCLUDING ENVIRONMENT VARIABLES

Using environment, or system, variables is a quick and easy way to include information in an HTML file in a dynamic fashion, especially when combined with other directives as will be discussed later on. Keep in mind that environment variables are system-dependent and that not all variables will be available on all machines, nor will they always have the same name. Consult your ISP or system administrator for the environment variable specifics of your server.

The following environment variables will be addressed in this chapter:

DATE_GMT	Date and time: Greenwich Mean Time.
DATE_LOCAL	Date and time: Local. (Local in this instance means local to the machine hosting the Web site, not the visitor looking at your page.)
DOCUMENT_NAME	The name of the current page.
HTTP_USER_AGENT	Your visitor's browser.
LAST_MODIFIED	The date and time a file was last modified.
REMOTE_ADDR	The IP address from which a visitor is accessing your page.
REMOTE_HOST	The host name from which a visitor is accessing your page.

The directive for including environment variables in a document is **echo.** An example using the variable HTTP_USER_AGENT would be:

```
<!--echo var="HTTP_USER_AGENT"-->
```

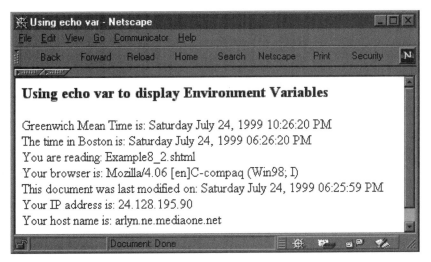

Figure 8.4 ■ Displaying environment variables.

Heed the fact that SSI syntax is extremely finicky and unforgiving. If it is not followed exactly, errors will occur, some of them quite nasty. Figure 8.4 shows how a Web page calling all of the above environment variables might look.

The output of the date variables, DATE_GMT and DATE_LOCAL, can be formatted to almost any style of presentation using the config timefmt directive. Note how the dates are listed by default in Figure 8.4. To change the presentation to, for instance, "24 July 99 - Saturday", the SSI code would be:

```
<!--#config timefmt="%d %B %y - %A"-->
```

The complete list of timefmt values is:

Value	Format	Example
%a	Day name – abbreviated	Sat
%A	Day name	Saturday
%b	Month name – abbreviated	Jul
%B	Month name	July
%d	Day of the month number	24
%D	Full numeric date	07/24/99
%e	Day of the month number-single digit	1 instead of 01
%H	24-hour clock hour	18

`%I`	12-hour clock hour	6
`%j`	Day of the year number	205
`%m`	Month number	07
`%M`	Minutes	26
`%p`	AM or PM	PM
`%I`	12-hour clock	06:26:20 PM
`%S`	Seconds	20
`%T`	24-hour clock	18:26:20
`%U`	Week of the year number	29
`%w`	Day of the week number (Sunday=0)	6
`%y`	Year of the century	99
`%Y`	Year	1999
`%Z`	Time zone	EST

LAB 8.2 EXERCISES

8.2.1 INCLUDING ENVIRONMENT VARIABLES

Write the code to include the following information in your HTML document:

a) The name of the document your visitor is reading.

_____

_____

b) The current local time in 24-hour clock format.

_____

_____

c) The GMT time as hours and minutes only.

_____

_____

d) The IP address of your visitor.

_____

_____

e) The host name of your visitor.

_____

_____

f) The browser your visitor is using.

_____

_____

g) The date the current file was last modified.

_____

_____

LAB 8.2 EXERCISE ANSWERS

8.2.1 ANSWERS

Write the code to include the following information in your HTML document:

a) The name of the document your visitor is reading.

Answer:

```
<!--#echo var="DOCUMENT_NAME"-->
```

b) The current local time in 24-hour clock format.

Answer:

```
<!--#config timefmt="%T"-->
<!--#echo var="DATE_LOCAL"-->
```

c) The GMT time as hours and minutes only.

Answer:

```
<!--#config timefmt="%H:%M %Z"-->
<!--#echo var="DATE_GMT"-->
```

d) The IP address of your visitor.

Answer:

```
<!--#echovar="REMOTE_ADDR"-->
```

e) The host name of your visitor.

Answer:

```
<!--#echo var="REMOTE_HOST"-->
```

f) The browser your visitor is using.

Answer:

```
<!--#echo var="HTTP_USER_AGENT"-->
```

g) The date the current file was last modified.

Answer:

```
<!--#echo var="LAST_MODIFIED"-->
```

LAB 8.2 SELF-REVIEW QUESTIONS

1) The environment variables discussed in this chapter are available on all platforms.
   a) True
   b) False

2) All ISPs allow SSIs to access all environment variables.
   a) True
   b) False

3) The command used to display an environment variable is
   a) exec
   b) include
   c) echo
   d) config

4) The command used to format date output is
   a) exec
   b) include
   c) echo
   d) config

5) Including DATE_LOCAL in an HTML document will render
   a) The current date and time where the visitor resides
   b) The current date and time where the Web site resides
   c) The current GMT date and time

Quiz answers appear in the Appendix, Section 8.2.

L A B   8 . 3

INCLUDING UNIX COMMANDS

As with environment variables, the UNIX commands available for execution via Server Side Includes will vary from system to system and are up to the discretion of your ISP or system administrator. You will need to check to see what commands, if any, are available for SSIs.

The directive for processing commands is **exec.** In the following example, the date command, which returns the current date and time in a format that is a slightly different format than the default format of the DATE_LOCAL environment variable, is issued.

```
<!--#exec cmd="date"-->
```

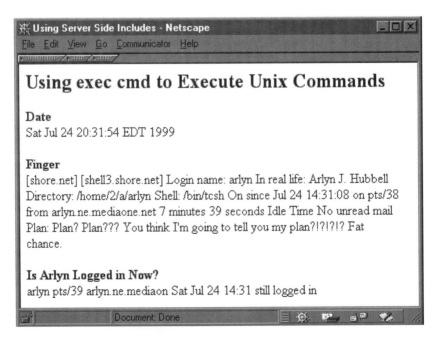

Figure 8.5 ■ Executing UNIX commands.

Figure 8.6 ■ The source code for Figure 8.5.

The output of `date` and two other UNIX commands is shown in Figure 8.5.

Note that the information returned by the `date` command cannot be re-formatted using `config timefmt`. The method you choose to retrieve time and date information for a Web page is strictly up to you and the re-sources available to you.

The remaining two commands processed in Figure 8.5 are `finger` and `last`. See Figure 8.6, the source code for Figure 8.5, for how the com-mands are issued using SSIs.

Figure 8.7 ■ `finger` output during a UNIX shell session.

`finger` displays various information about a shell account user if the command is enabled on the server. It is included in this example to demonstrate the difference between how the display of returned information may differ between a Web page and when the command is issued at the UNIX prompt. From the UNIX prompt `finger arlyn@shore.net` generates output as seen in Figure 8.7. Compare this to what the command displays by default in Figure 8.5. While all the information is indeed there and the visitor can, if they have the patience, read it, the format is not pretty.

LAB
8.3

The `last` command, shown in Figure 8.5, displays information about a user's shell history. In this case, the command shows the last login for `arlyn`, and the output indicates that the user `arlyn` was still logged in at the time the Web page was accessed.

LAB 8.4

INCLUDING EXTERNAL FILES

The use of the SSI directive **include** allows you to pull the content of another file into the current HTML file. The syntax of the directive is as follows:

```
<!--#include file="anotherfile"-->
```

Note that the file you wish to include in the file containing the directive does not necessarily need to be another HTML file.

While the directive itself is fairly straightforward, it is worthwhile to take a look at a couple of examples of its use. To start, examine Figure 8.8, a simple Web page formatted into two columns using borderless tables.

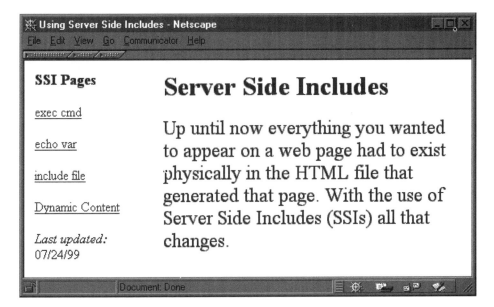

Figure 8.8 ■ Using include file.

The left column is a sidebar-style index for the small site and the right column is straight content.

Viewing the source code with a browser would show nothing but the HTML used to generate the window's page. In actuality though, the source code for the left-hand table cell is:

```
<TD WIDTH="30%">
<!--#include file="contents.shtml"-->
</TD>
```

That's it. The directive `include file` tells the server to insert the contents of `contents.shtml` into the table cell. The contents of the included file is:

```
<H3>SSI Pages</H3>
<A HREF="Example8_1.shtml">exec cmd</A>
<BR><BR>
<A HREF="Example8_2.shtml">echo var</A>
<BR><BR>
<A HREF="Example8_3.shtml">include file</A>
<BR><BR>
<A HREF="Example8_6.shtml">Dynamic Content</A>
<BR><BR>
<!--#config timefmt="%D"-->
<I>
Last updated:<BR>
</I>
<!--#echo var="LAST_MODIFIED"-->
```

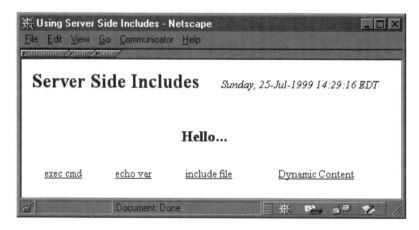

Figure 8.9 ■ Using `include file` to include a header and footer.

Note that `contents.shtml` does not contain the usual HTML, HEAD, TITLE, and BODY tags. As a rule, these tags should not be used in HTML files destined to be included in other HTML files—they will only cause problems.

Another example of the use of SSIs is to include headers and footers in Web pages as is illustrated in Figure 8.9.

The beauty of the `include file` directive is that it makes it very easy for a Web author to set up a library of page templates and universal content files, such as headers, footers, and indexes, which are included in the templates using SSIs. Then, when new Web pages need to be created, all the author needs to do is select the proper template, copy it to a new file, and modify it with the unique content for that page.

LAB 8.4 EXERCISE

8.4.1 INCLUDING EXTERNAL FILES

The source code for the Web page in Figure 8.9 is contains 12 lines. **Hello...** is the only content physically contained in the `.shtml` file. The rest of the HTML and content are contained in two external files:

`header.shtml:`

```
<TABLE WIDTH="100%">
<TR>
<TD ALIGN=LEFT>
<H2>Server Side Includes</H2>
</TD>
<TD ALIGN=RIGHT VALIGN=BASELINE>
<I><SMALL><!--#echo var="LAST_MODIFIED"--></SMALL></I>
</TD>
</TR>
</TABLE>
```

and `footer.shtml:`

```
<CENTER>
<TABLE WIDTH="100%">
<TR ALIGN=CENTER>
<TD>
<A HREF="Example8_1.shtml"><SMALL>exec
cmd</SMALL></A>
</TD>
<TD>
<A HREF="Example8_2.shtml"><SMALL>echo
var</SMALL></A>
</TD>
<TD>
<A HREF="Example8_3.shtml"><SMALL>include
file</SMALL></A>
</TD>
<TD>
<A HREF="Example8_6.shtml"><SMALL>Dynamic
Content</SMALL></A>
</TD>
</TR>
</TABLE>
</CENTER>
</BODY>
</HTML>
```

Review the page and write the source code that would generate the page in Figure 8.9.

LAB 8.4 EXERCISE ANSWER

8.4.1 ANSWER

Review the page and write the source code that would generate the page in Figure 8.9.

Answer: The source code for Figure 8.9 is:

```
<HTML>
<HEAD>
<TITLE>Using Server Side Includes</TITLE>
</HEAD>
<BODY BGCOLOR="#ffffff">
<!--#include file="header.shtml"-->
<CENTER><H3> Hello… </H3></CENTER>
```

```
<!--#include file="footer.shtml"-->
</BODY>
</HTML>
```

LAB 8.4 SELF-REVIEW QUESTIONS

1) All UNIX commands are available for execution via SSIs.
    a) True
    b) False
    c) Varies from system to system

2) HTML files that are created for the sole purpose of being included in other HTML files should not contain HTML, HEAD, TITLE, and BODY elements.
    a) True
    b) False

3) HTML files meant for inclusion in other HTML files may not contain additional SSIs.
    a) True
    b) False

Quiz answers appear in the Appendix, Section 8.4.

L A B   8 . 5

USING ENVIRONMENT VARIABLES FOR DYNAMIC PAGE GENERATION

Things start to get really interesting when SSIs and environment variables are used to create dynamic Web pages, pages that have varying content depending on which environment variable is examined and the information it returns. Pages can be customized on-the-fly to accommodate host names, IP addresses, the date and/or time, and the browser or platform your visitor is using to view the page.

Suppose we wanted to change the content of a page according to the IP address of a visitor? This can be done, with a little effort, by testing environment variable REMOTE_ADDR for certain information with the **if** directive. To illustrate, the following source code produces the two different pages shown in Figures 8.10 and 8.11 depending on the visitor's IP address:

```
<HTML>
<HEAD>
<TITLE>Using Server Side Includes</TITLE>
</HEAD>
<BODY BGCOLOR="#ffffff">
<!--#include file="header.shtml"-->
<H6 style="color:#ffffff">
<!--#echo var="REMOTE_ADDR"-->
</H6>
<!--#if expr="$REMOTE_ADDR=/24.128.195.*/"-->
<CENTER>
<H3> Welcome. </H3>
```

```
<BR>
</CENTER>
<CENTER>
<!--#include file="footer.shtml"-->
</CENTER>
<!--#else -->
<CENTER>
<H3>I'm sorry. This page is restricted.</H3>
</CENTER>
<BR>
<!--endif -->
</BODY>
</HTML>
```

If we know that the IP addresses of welcome visitors start with 24.128.95, we can look for that string in REMOTE_ADDRESS with the following directive:

```
<!--#if expr=$REMOTE_ADDR=/24.128.195.*/"-->
```

The admissible audience could be increased by testing for 24.128.*.*, or even 24.*.*.*. On the other hand, you could test for a single user or machine by making the IP address more specific: 24.128.195.90. The asterisks serve as wildcards, or placeholders. When they are present, any number can replace them and the test would be positive.

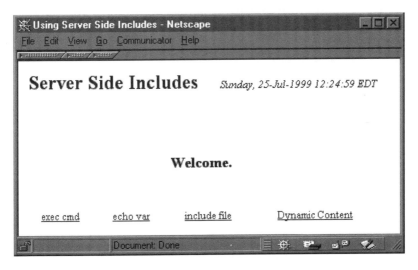

Figure 8.10 ■ The IP address is accepted.

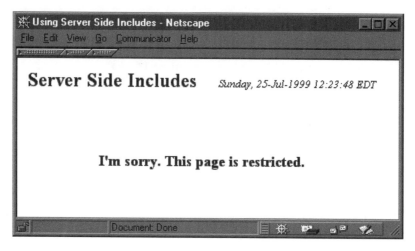

Figure 8.11 ■ **The IP address is not accepted.**

The **else** directive indicates what should be displayed if the IP address does not match the string in the **if** statement. **endif** concludes the testing process. Anything that appears after **endif** will be displayed regardless of the visitor's IP address.

It needs to be mentioned that this technique of filtering visitors to your Web site does not qualify as any level of security. A couple of bona fide security strategies will be discussed in Chapter 9.

We can make a page even more dynamic by testing for other factors and including additional page content based on the results of the tests. To continue with the example we've already started, think about how you might go about testing for the day of the week and presenting page content based on the day. Perhaps you have a message of the day to present, or daily schedules or task lists to publish.

The **elif** directive is required to do this. Remembering that DATE_LOCAL is accessed in the header file, the augmented testing code might look like this:

```
<!--#include file="header.shtml"-->
<H6 style="color:#ffffff">
<!--#echo var="REMOTE_ADDR"-->
</H6>
<!--#if expr="$REMOTE_ADDR=/24.128.195.*/ &&
$DATE_LOCAL=/Sunday/"-->
        <CENTER><H3> Welcome. </H3></CENTER>
        <!--#include file="sunday"-->
        <!--#include file="footer.shtml"-->
```

```
<!--#elif expr="$REMOTE_ADDR=/24.128.195.*/ &&
$DATE_LOCAL=/Monday/"-->
<CENTER><H3> Welcome. </H3></CENTER>
        <!--#include file="monday"-->
        <!--#include file="footer.shtml"-->
<!--#elif expr="$REMOTE_ADDR=/24.128.195.*/ &&
$DATE_LOCAL=/Tuesday/"-->
<CENTER><H3> Welcome. </H3></CENTER>
        <!--#include file="tuesday"-->
        <!--#include file="footer.shtml"-->
<!--#elif expr="$REMOTE_ADDR=/24.128.195.*/ &&
$DATE_LOCAL=/Wednesday/"-->
<CENTER><H3> Welcome. </H3></CENTER>
<!--#include file="wednesday"-->
        <!--#include file="footer.shtml"-->
<!--#elif expr="$REMOTE_ADDR=/24.128.195.*/ &&
$DATE_LOCAL=/Thursday/"-->
<CENTER><H3> Welcome. </H3></CENTER>
        <!--#include file="thursday"-->
        <!--#include file="footer.shtml"-->
<!--#elif expr="$REMOTE_ADDR=/24.128.195.*/ &&
$DATE_LOCAL=/Friday/"-->
<CENTER><H3> Welcome. </H3></CENTER>
        <!--#include file="friday"-->
        <!--#include file="footer.shtml"-->
<!--#elif expr="$REMOTE_ADDR=/24.128.195.*/ &&
$DATE_LOCAL=/Saturday/"-->
<CENTER><H3> Welcome. </H3></CENTER>
        <!--#include file="saturday"-->
        <!--#include file="footer.shtml"-->
<!--#elif expr="$REMOTE_ADDR=/*.*.*.*/"-->
<CENTER><H2>I'm sorry. I don't have anything for
you.</H2></CENTER>
<!--#endif -->
```

**LAB
8.5**

This is without a doubt the most elegant way to code the testing sequence, but perhaps it is not clear. You will notice that after the first **if** statement, **elif** is used for the balance of the conditions tested. **elif** is the same as else. The conditions look for a valid IP address and (**&&**) the name of the date in DATE_LOCAL. If both requirements are met, the hunt through the conditions stops and content is displayed (Figure 8.12). The last **elif** statement:

```
<!--#elif expr="$REMOTE_ADDR=/*.*.*.*/"-->
```

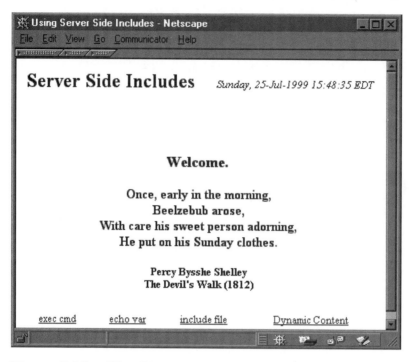

Figure 8.12 ■ **The IP address matches and the day is Sunday.**

acts as a broad catch-all for anything that does not match the specified parameters and, as a courtesy, includes default content for display (Figure 8.13).

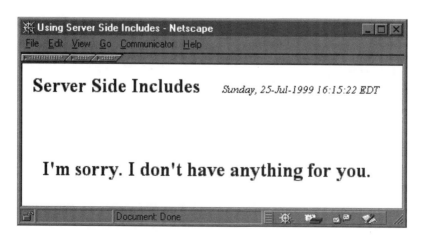

Figure 8.13 ■ **A default message for when no parameters are matched.**

LAB 8.5 EXERCISES

8.5.1 USING ENVIRONMENT VARIABLES FOR DYNAMIC PAGE GENERATION

Write the SSI code to test for the following conditions and display content accordingly:

a) Check the date to see if it is July. If it is, the page displays: **It's July!** If it isn't, the page displays: **It isn't July!**

_____

_____

b) Write a statement that will allow a visitor with the IP address 24.128.195.90 to see specific information on your page.

_____

_____

c) Modify the above statement to display information if the IP address is 24.128.195.90 and it is July.

_____

_____

d) Whereas **&&** means "and," **||** means "or." Write the condition that will allow people from IP addresses starting with 24.128 or 198.204 to see content on your page.

_____

_____

LAB 8.5 EXERCISE ANSWERS

8.5.1 ANSWERS

a) Check the date to see if it is July. If it is, the page displays: **It's July!** If it isn't, the page displays: **It isn't July!**

Answer:

```
<HTML>
<HEAD>
<TITLE>Test</TITLE>
</HEAD>
<BODY BGCOLOR="#ffffff">
<H6 style="color:#ffffff">
<!--#echo var="DATE_LOCAL"-->
</H6>
<!--#if expr="$DATE_LOCAL=/Jul/"-->
<H1>It's July!</H1>
<!--#else -->
<H1>It isn't July!</H1>
<!--#endif -->
</BODY>
</HTML>
```

b) Write a statement that will allow a visitor with the IP address 24.128.195.90 to see specific information on your page.

Answer:

```
<!--#if expr="$REMOTE_ADDR=/24.128.195.90/"-->
```

c) Modify the above statement to display information if the IP address is 24.128.195.90 and it is July.

Answer:

```
<!--#if expr="$REMOTE_ADDR=/24.128.195.90/ &&
$DATE_LOCAL=/Jul/"-->
```

d) Whereas **&&** means "and," **||** means "or." Write the condition that will allow people from IP addresses starting with 24.128 or 198.204 to see content on your page.

Answer:

```
<!--#if expr="$REMOTE_ADDR=/24.128.*.*/" ||
$REMOTE_ADDR="$REMOTE_ADDR=/198.204.*.*"-->
```

LAB 8.5 SELF-REVIEW QUESTIONS

1) Wildcards may be used to test for blocks of IP addresses.
  a) True
  b) False

2) Only one environment variable may be tested at a time.
  a) True
  b) False

3) SSIs may be used as a means of restricting Web page access.
  a) True
  b) False

4) More than one condition may be tested at a time.
  a) True
  b) False

Quiz answers appear in the Appendix, Section 8.5.

LAB
8.5

C H A P T E R   8

TEST YOUR THINKING

The projects in this section use the skills you've acquired in this chapter. The answers to these projects are available to instructors only through a Prentice Hall sales representative and are intended to be used in classroom discussion and assessment.

A lot of ground has been covered in this chapter. Think about what you have seen and how you might use Server Side Includes to enhance your Web site.

1) Set up a template .shtml file that will include external header and footer files.

2) Create a header that displays the current date and time and a graphic that is selected based on the day of the week.

3) Create a footer that displays an appropriate set of links based on the visitor's IP address.

CHAPTER 9

RESTRICTING WEB SITE ACCESS WITH .HTACCESS

 A sekret ceases to be a sekret if it iz once confided—it iz like a dollar bill, once broken, it iz never a dollar agin.

Josh Billings
[Henry Wheeler Shaw]
Affurisms (1865)

CHAPTER OBJECTIVES

In this chapter, you will learn about:

A good rule of thumb to remember is: If you do not want information to be available to the world, do not put it on the Web. The Web, by default, is a vehicle for making content available to everyone regardless of who they are, where they are, or the software and platform they might be using.

There are, however, ways to secure information to a certain extent, and one method is to use the Apache server's .htaccess file.

LAB 9.1

HOW THE .HTACCESS FILE WORKS

The .htaccess file (an example of a "dot" file, mentioned in Chapter 1) is a set of instructions, or directives, to be used by the Apache Web server while processing requests for data from your HTML directories. The file is created using the text editor of your choice and placed within the directory that requires special processing. Be certain, when creating the file, to set permissions on the file so that it is readable by the world. Otherwise, the file will render the directory inaccessible by a browser. If the file is located at the top level of your Web site, .htaccess instructions and protection will apply to the main directory and all of its subdirectories. Locating an .htaccess file within a subdirectory causes the file's instructions to be processed only when that directory and its subdirectories are accessed.

It should be mentioned here that using .htaccess to limit access to areas of your Web site should not be considered a flawless form of security, and that should be made clear to your prospective clients when discussing the utility. It does, however, provide an effective initial means of protecting directories from unwanted visitors. It should also be noted that the .htaccess file's instructions work at a directory level and, for our purposes here, cannot protect individual files.

L A B   9 . 2

LIMITING WEB PAGE ACCESS BY REMOTE ADDRESS

The `allow` and `deny` directives facilitate access and nonaccess to a Web site directory by remote address, the address of your visitor. This can be done from a very broad level, for instance, limiting a directory's access to only `.edu` sites, down to a very specific level, such as restricting a single machine address from viewing the directory.

There are a number of reasons for employing this sort of access limitation, but popular examples include:

- Restricting use of installed software to a single domain hierarchy. For instance, you may have a utility on your site that may be used without charge by educational institutions only. Restricting your site or the directory containing the utility to .edu addresses only is one way to enforce the rule to a degree that will be acceptable to the software vendor.
- Companies may wish to make information available to visitors coming from a single remote address or a known list of remote addresses, but may not want to go so far as to require user IDs and passwords.
- A company might want to allow access to everyone but visitors coming from the remote address of a certain competitor.
- On an intranet, or an internal Web site, you may wish to restrict a directory's access from a certain group of machines, for instance, a set of public machines that may be supplied as a courtesy to office visitors.

ALLOWING ACCESS

The following is an `.htaccess` file that allows access to visitors coming only from `arlyn.com`:

```
AuthType Basic

<Limit>
order deny,allow
deny from all
allow from .arlyn.com
</Limit>
```

The directive `AuthType` sets the authorization to `Basic`, the only authorization type implemented by Apache at this time. The `Limit` directive encloses the rules by which the directory is to be limited. In this case, without getting into too many details, access is denied to all but those coming from remote addresses ending with `arlyn.com`. Access could be broadened even further by changing `.arlyn.com` to `.com`, which would allow the directory to be viewed by anyone coming from a remote address ending in `.com`. A visitor from an address that does not fit the rules as stated in the above example will receive an Error 403 message as shown in Figure 9.1.

DENYING ACCESS

The logic in the above example can be reversed to deny access to anyone coming in from `arlyn.com`, causing them to receive the Error 403 message shown in Figure 9.1:

Figure 9.1 ■ **Access denied by a restricted directory.**

```
AuthType Basic

<Limit GET>
order allow,deny
allow from all
deny from .arlyn.com
</Limit>
```

Note the change in the sequence of the order, allow, and deny rules and how they change arlyn.com's access rights to the given directory. Again, the deny access can be made more inclusive by changing .arlyn.com to .com. We can also allow and deny access from multiple remote addresses by listing them, separated by commas as follows:

```
deny from .arlyn.com, .arlyn.net
```

    or

```
allow from .arlyn.com, .arlyn.net
```

LAB 9.2 EXERCISES

9.2.1 LIMITING WEB DIRECTORY ACCESS BY REMOTE ADDRESS

a) Write the access file that will deny access to a directory from all visitors coming from prenhall.com.

_____

_____

b) Write the access file that will allow access to a directory to visitors from prenhall.com only.

_____

_____

c) Modify the appropriate directives in the above files so they will respectively deny and allow access to visitors from all .com sites.

_____

_____

d) Modify the directives again so that the files will deny and allow access from all `.com` visitors and all visitors from `arlyn.net`.

LAB 9.2 EXERCISE ANSWERS

9.2.1 ANSWERS

a) Write the access file that will deny access to a directory from all visitors coming from `prenhall.com`.

Answer: `AuthType Basic`

```
<Limit GET>
order allow,deny
allow from all
deny from .prenhall.com
</Limit>
```

b) Write the access file that will allow access to a directory to visitors from `prenhall.com` only.

Answer: `AuthType Basic`

```
<Limit>
order deny,allow
deny from all
allow from .prenhall.com
</Limit>
```

c) Modify the appropriate directives in the above files so they will respectively deny and allow access to visitors from all .com sites.

Answer: `deny from .com`

   `allow from .com`

d) Modify the directives again so that the files will deny and allow access from all `.com` visitors and all visitors from `arlyn.net`.

Answer: `deny from .com, arlyn.net`

   `allow from .com, arlyn.net`

LAB 9.2 SELF-REVIEW QUESTIONS

1) The file containing the directives which limit access to Web site directories is called
    a) .htaccess
    b) htaccess
    c) htaccess.

2) An access file located in a subdirectory will protect the entire Web site according to the directives within the file.
    a) True
    b) False

3) The directive `deny from .users.arlyn.com` will
    a) Prevent a machine called `users.arlyn.com` from accessing a directory
    b) Prevent anyone from `users.arlyn.com` from accessing a directory
    c) Both of the above
    d) Neither of the above

4) A visitor who has been denied access to a restricted directory will receive
    a) An Error 401 message
    b) An Error 403 message
    c) An Error 404 message
    d) None of the above

Quiz answers appear in the Appendix, Section 9.2.

L A B   9 . 3

PASSWORD-PROTECTING WEB DIRECTORIES

Password protection is another means of limiting access to your various directories. Again, the reasons for securing information in this fashion are unlimited, but common scenarios include:

- Closing areas of a Web site that are "under development."
- Securing proprietary information and allowing use to a known population of users.
- Creating discreet and private directories for individual customers.

Setting up password protection is a two-step process, the first of which is the creation of a simple `.htaccess` file in the directory that needs to be protected:

```
AuthName "Secrets"
AuthType Basic
AuthUserFile /home/web/webclass.merrimack.edu/users

require valid-user
```

`AuthName` identifies the realm of authorization for the client, or browser. In this case, `.htaccess` is located in a directory called `secrets`, hence the choice of the name "`Secrets`". `AuthType` sets the type of user authorization as before.

`AuthUserFile` indicates the location and name of the file containing allowed user IDs and encrypted passwords. This must be specified using the full path, or complete directory address, of the file. It does not matter what you name the file, but it must be readable by the world and it is recom-

Figure 9.2 ■ A request for a user ID and password from a protected site.

mended that it be located in a directory that **cannot** be browsed via the Web so that curious visitors will not be able to obtain a list of valid user IDs.

The `require` directive states that a valid user ID and password from the `AuthUserFile` are needed to view the files in the directory.

Upon entering the URL for a password-protected directory, the unauthenticated user is presented with an opportunity to enter their user ID and password as seen in Figure 9.2.

At this point, your visitor will enter a user ID and password. If they are correct, entrance is allowed into the protected area and the appropriate HTML page is displayed. If an incorrect ID and password are entered, the visitor will receive an authorization failure message similar to the one shown in Figure 9.3. Figure 9.4 is an example of the Error 401 message that is generated by default if the visitor cancels or closes the login process.

The second step to password-protecting a directory in this fashion is to create the user file you have listed in the `AuthUserFile` directive. This is done with the program `htpasswd`, which is available on most Apache servers. To create a new password file, telnet to your Web site's server, log in, change directory to where the file is to reside, and issue the following command:

Figure 9.3 ■ A password authorization failure message.

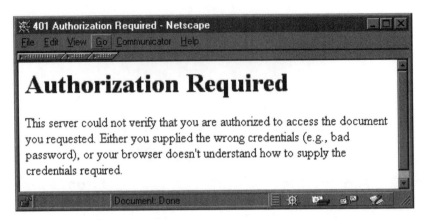

Figure 9.4 ■ Error 401.

```
htpasswd -c file-name first-userid
```

The program will create the new password file and query you for the password for the first user ID. The entire session to create the password file for the directory `secrets` looked like this:

```
webclass.merrimack.edu% htpasswd -c users arlyn
Adding password for arlyn.
New password:
Re-type new password:
webclass.merrimack.edu%
```

Do not forget that your password file must be world-readable, and must be set as such using `chmod` when it is first created.

Additional users and passwords can be added by invoking `htpasswd` without the `-c` flag as follows:

```
webclass.merrimack.edu% htpasswd users carl
Adding user carl
New password:
Re-type new password:
webclass.merrimack.edu%
```

A user password can be changed by invoking `htpasswd` with an existing user ID:

```
webclass.merrimack.edu% htpasswd users carl
```

```
Changing password for user carl
New password:
Re-type new password:
webclass.merrimack.edu%
```

To remove a user ID entirely, you will need to manually edit your password file and delete the line containing the user ID and password.

Password protection can be a somewhat confusing process at first, but you must not let it daunt you. Once you've set up a few directories successfully, it will be a simple, straightforward, and extremely useful tool to have in your repertoire.

**LAB
9.3**

L A B   9 . 4

USING .HTACCESS TO ACCESS CUSTOM ERROR PAGES

While they are not directly a part of limiting access, it is a nice touch to create custom error pages to be displayed when people are denied access to restricted areas of your Web site. For instance, the Web site containing the restricted directories discussed in this chapter includes the custom pages shown in Figure 9.5 for Error 403 (Access Forbidden) and Figure 9.6 for Error 401 (Authorization Required).

While the examples here are very simple, you can see how they are much friendlier than the default pages provided by the Apache server. Also, they allow you to include additional information for the user who may be having problems, such as whom to contact for help—in this case, an email link to the site's Webmaster, as well as appropriate company logos and graphics.

The actual pages are created in the same manner as the rest of your Web pages. They are then called using the `ErrorDocument` directive in an `.htaccess` file as follows:

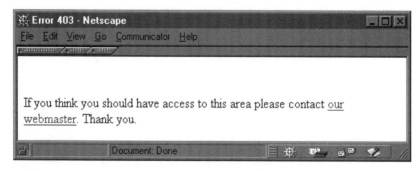

Figure 9.5 ■ A custom error 403 page.

Figure 9.6 ■ A custom error 401 page.

```
ErrorDocument  401  /ahubbell/error401.html
ErrorDocument  403  /ahubbell/error403.html
ErrorDocument  404  /ahubbell/error404.html
```

The syntax of the directive is the server error number, in this case 401, 403, or 404 (File not Found), followed by the location and name of the HTML file to be displayed when the error occurs. Note that the file location is written relative to the root of the URL from which it will be called. In this chapter, the root of the URL for all of the directories created is `webclass.merrimack.edu`, therefore the URL for the Error 401 page listed above is `webclass.merrimack.edu/ahubbell/error401.html`.

LAB 9.4 EXERCISES

9.4.1 USING .HTACCESS TO ACCESS CUSTOM ERROR PAGES

a) Write the `.htaccess` file necessary to password-protect a directory called `Clients`. The file containing user IDs and passwords is called `access`, and it is located in `/home1/users/mysite`.

_____

_____

b) Write the command to create the password file `Clients` and add the user `thomas`.

_____

_____

c) Write the command to change the password for user `thomas`.

_____

_____

d) Write the directive that will display `badpassword.html` to users who do not have a valid ID and password for a protected site. `Badpassword.html` is located in subdirectory `custpages`.

_____

_____

LAB 9.4 EXERCISE ANSWERS

9.4.1 ANSWERS

a) Write the .htaccess file necessary to password-protect a directory called `Clients`. The file containing user IDs and passwords is called `access`, and it is located in `/home1/users/mysite`.

Answer: `AuthName "Secrets"`
`        AuthType Basic`
`        AuthUserFile /home1/users/mysite/Clients`

`        require valid-user`

b) Write the command to create the password file Clients and add the user `thomas`.

Answer: `htpasswd -c Clients thomas`

c) Write the command to change the password for user `thomas`.

Answer: `htpasswd Clients thomas`

d) Write the directive that will display `badpassword.html` to users who do not have a valid ID and password for a protected site. `Badpassword.html` is located in subdirectory `custpages`.

Answer: `ErrorDocument 401 /custpages/badpassword.html`

LAB 9.4 SELF-REVIEW QUESTIONS

1) Password protection using `.htaccess` provides a site with absolute security.
   a) True
   b) False

2) User IDs and passwords should be kept in a file that is browsable via the Web.
   a) True
   b) False

3) `.htaccess` can be used to password-protect one specific file within a directory.
   a) True
   b) False

4) The command to remove the user ID `thomas` from the password file `Clients` is `htpasswd -d Clients thomas`.
   a) True
   b) False

Quiz answers appear in the Appendix, Section 9.4.

**LAB
9.4**

C H A P T E R   9

TEST YOUR THINKING

The projects in this section use the skills you've acquired in this chapter. The answers to these projects are available to instructors only through a Prentice Hall sales representative and are intended to be used in classroom discussion and assessment.

As stated earlier, the best way to become fluent with the concepts involved in restricting access to areas of your Web sites is to use the techniques. Create three new directories in the Web site you have been working on while reading this book.

1) Allow access to the first based on the visitor's remote address.

2) Deny access to the second based on the visitor's remote access.

3) Password protect the third directory and add four valid user IDs to a file called "Friends." Create a custom page that will be displayed if a visitor does not have a valid ID and password.

CHAPTER 10

A BRIEF INTRODUCTION TO STYLE SHEETS

Style is the dress of thoughts.

Philip Dormer Stanhope, Earl of Chesterfield
Letters (1749)

CHAPTER OBJECTIVES

In this chapter, you will learn about:

✔ The anatomy of style	Page 233
✔ Three methods of incorporating style into an HTML document	Page 238
✔ Basic style properties and values	Page 241
✔ Space properties and values	Page 248

While Web browsers since day one have used HTML style sheets to interpret HTML elements, they weren't available for the general use of Web designers until early 1997. And the designers were thrilled. They were able to position the elements of a page to the absolute pixel. Text could be formatted with margins and indentation, without the use of cumbersome tables. Best of all, all of the style instructions for a Web site could be included in a few style sheets which could then be linked to from any number of HTML pages. Thus, when site-wide appearance changes had to be made, they could be made in the style sheets instead of every single HTML file.

On the downside, the browsers were not, and still are not, in agreement as to how different elements of style should be interpreted or even if they should be interpreted at all. What might be beautiful when looked at with one browser might be less so with another, and possibly a disaster with yet another.

Keep in mind while working with style sheets that, as much fun as adding style can be, it is still the content that counts most. Style is the dress of content.

L A B   1 0 . 1

THE ANATOMY
OF STYLE

Take a look at the Web pages presented in Figures 10.1 and 10.2. Both of them use the exact same HTML elements to present identical content, yet you will notice quite a difference in presentation. Margins, justified text, paragraph indentation, and an italicized header are all found in Figure 10.2, without the use of any tables or additional attributes in the HTML elements. The culprit is known as a style sheet, which is a few lines of specialized code included within the STYLE elements inside the header of Figure 10.2's HTML document:

```
<STYLE>
BODY {background-color:#ffffff;
      color:#000000;
      margin-left:8%
      }
```

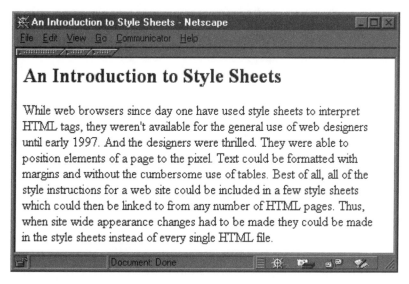

Figure 10.1 ■ A standard Web page.

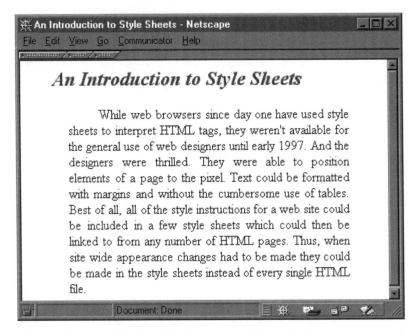

Figure 10.2 ■ Figure 10.1's Web page with style incorporated.

```
H2     { color:#800080;
         font-style:italic
         }

P      { text-indent:2em;
         margin-left:5%;
         margin-right:10%;
         text-align:justify
         }
</STYLE>
```

Simply put, a style sheet is nothing but a set of instructions for rendering HTML elements, something every browser already has by default. By including style attributes in an HTML file, the browser's default style is overridden to the extent that the browser is able to display the content as instructed, assuming that the owner of the browser has not disabled style sheets in the preferences.

A single instruction, for instance, P {text-indent:2em}, is referred to as a Rule. The Rule contains two parts: the Selector and the Declaration. The Selector is the HTML element to which author-specified effects are to be applied. The Declaration specifies how the Selector should be rendered.

P   **{text-indent:2em}**
The Selector   The Declaration

You will notice in the example above that the P Selector actually has four Declarations, separated by semi-colons. This is called grouping Declarations.

The Declaration in turn is comprised of two parts: the Property and the Value. The Property is the aspect of a Selector to be affected. The Value is how the Property aspect should be rendered. A colon always separates the Property and Value, as semi-colons always separate grouped Declarations. Omission of either punctuation will cause a browser to ignore the Declaration, and possibly the entire Rule, completely.

{text-indent: 2em}
The Property   The Value

This Rule states that the first line of a paragraph should be indented 2 ems. Regardless of how you choose to incorporate style into your HTML documents, you will always be working with Selectors, Properties, and Values.

LAB 10.1 EXERCISES

10.1.1   THE ANATOMY OF STYLE

a) When were style sheets first made available to HTML authors?

_____

_____

b) A style sheet instruction is referred to as a Rule. What are the two parts that comprise a Rule?

_____

_____

c) What two parts make up a Declaration?

_____

_____

d) The Rule is: `H2{color:#800080}`. Label the individual parts of the Rule.

`color:`

`H2`

`#8000800`

LAB 10.1 EXERCISE ANSWERS

10.1.1 ANSWERS

a) When were Style Sheets first made available to HTML authors?

Answer: Early 1997

b) A style sheet instruction is referred to as a Rule. What are the two parts that comprise a Rule?

Answer: 1. The Selector

2. The Declaration

c) What two parts make up a Declaration?

Answer: 1. The Property

2. The Value

d) The Rule is: `H2 {color:#8000800}`. Label the individual parts of the rule.

Answer: `color:`   *The Property*

`H2`   *The Selector*

`#800080`   *The Value*

LAB 10.1 SELF-REVIEW QUESTIONS

1) Prior to 1997, style sheets were not used.
   a) True
   b) False

2) Multiple Declarations for a single Selector must be separated by
   a) Commas
   b) Colons
   c) Semi-colons

3) Within a Declaration, the Property and Value are separated by a
   a) Comma
   b) Colon
   c) Semi-colon

4) Browsers are in agreement as to how and when style Declarations should be interpreted.
   a) True
   b) False

Quiz answers appear in the Appendix, Section 10.1.

L A B   1 0 . 2

THREE METHODS OF INCORPORATING STYLE INTO AN HTML DOCUMENT

There are three ways to include style in your HTML documents, two of which you have seen already. Style instructions can be included within STYLE elements inside the header of a document or individual HTML elements, or they can be contained in an external document which is linked to from an HTML file.

INCLUDING STYLE WITH THE STYLE ELEMENT

This method of including style is seen in the source code for Figure 10.2. All style instructions are included within the STYLE inside the header of the document. The complete HTML file for Figure 10.1, minus the header and paragraph text, is:

```
<HTML>
<HEAD>
<TITLE>An Introduction to Style Sheets</TITLE>
<STYLE>
BODY {background-color:#ffffff;
      color:#000000;
      margin-left:8%
      }

H2    {color:#800080;
       font-style:italic
       }

P     {text-indent:2em;
```

```
            margin-left:5%;
            margin-right:10%;
            text-align:justify
          }

</STYLE>
</HEAD>
<BODY>
<H2> ...</H2>
<P>
...
</P>
</BODY>
</HTML>
```

This method of style inclusion is most often used for more than a few style instructions that are to be applied to a single HTML document. In this case, style is being set for the BODY, H2, and P elements.

INCLUDING STYLE IN HTML ELEMENTS

A style trick was used in the source code for Figures 8.10 and 8.11. For the H6 element, the text color is set to white so that the results of #echo var will not be seen on the Web page: `<H6  style="color:#ffffff">`. When style is added to a document using this method, it only applies to the element that contains the Declaration. Future occurrences of the same element will be displayed with its default property values, unless they are modified as well.

This method can also be used to override any previously declared styles for any one occurrence of an HTML element. For instance, in the code for Figure 10.2, the color for all H2 headers has been set to purple. If, later on in the document, an H2 header needs to be green, one way to do it would be:

```
    <H2 STYLE="color:green">A Green H2</H2>
```

The last Rule set for any HTML element is what will be used to render the text. So, if an attached external style sheet sets H2 headers to blue for Figure 10.2, the Rule within the STYLE elements would overrule it, making all H2 headers purple. The example above, included in the HTML, would in turn override the purple Rule for one instance only.

The source code for Figure 10.2, rewritten to include style Declarations within the HTML elements, minus header and paragraph content, looks like this:

```
<HTML>
<HEAD>
<TITLE>An Introduction to Style Sheets</TITLE>
</HEAD>

<BODY STYLE="background-color:#ffffff;
            color:#000000; margin-left:8%">

<H2 STYLE="color:#800080; font-style:italic"> …</H2>

<P STYLE="text-indent:2em; margin-left:5%;
        margin-right:10%; text-align:justify">

…
</P>
</BODY>
</HTML>
```

LINKING TO AN EXTERNAL STYLE SHEET

The last method of including style in an HTML document is to link to an external style sheet that includes Rules that can be applied to any number of Web pages. For instance, if the style Rules for Figure 10.2 were located in a file called `style1.css`, the style sheet could be linked to from an HTML document (assuming both files resided in the same directory) with the following code:

```
<HEAD>
<LINK REL=STYLESHEET TYPE="text/css"
HREF="style1.css">
</HEAD>
```

Again, the benefit of this method of incorporating style is that any number of HTML files can use one style sheet. Style that applies to a Web site as a whole resides in a few external files and individual rules are overridden with special cases in the HTML files.

L A B   1 0 . 3

BASIC STYLE PROPERTIES AND VALUES

Entire books have been written about style sheets and this chapter is not meant to replace a more thorough study of the subject that would include detailed discussions of fonts, space layout, and positioning. It is an *introduction*, and the hope is that you will learn enough about the basics to start using them to create more sophisticated Web pages when appropriate.

The following discussion of style Properties and Values is by no means all-inclusive, but it should get you started. At present, style sheets cause more browser compatibility headaches than almost any other facet of Web design. So that you can see the differences in display at even the simplest levels, example style pages are shown rendered by both Netscape 4.06 and Internet Explorer 5.00.

FONT PROPERTIES

The source code for the styles rendered in Figures 10.3 and 10.4 is:

```
<HTML>
<HEAD>
<TITLE>An Introduction to Style Sheets</TITLE>
<STYLE>
BODY {background-color:#ffffff;
     color:#000000;
     margin-left:8%;
     font-family:Arial, Helvetica, sans-serif
     }

H2    {color:#800080;
      font-style:italic;
```

```
                    margin-left:5%
                    }

        H3      {color:#000000;
                 font-style:oblique;
                 text-decoration:overline;
                 margin-left:8%
                 }

        H4      {color:#000000;
                 font-style:normal;
                 text-decoration:line-through;
                 margin-left:8%
                 }

        H5      {color:#000000;
                 font-style:normal;
                 text-decoration:underline;
                 margin-left:8%
                 }

        H6      {color:#000000;
                 font-style:normal;
                 font-weight:900;
                 margin-left:8%
                 }

        P       {text-indent:2em;
                 margin-left:5%;
                 margin-right:10%;
                 text-align:justify;
                 text-transform:capitalize
                 }

        </STYLE>
        </HEAD>
```

font-family   Used to specify an element's font set.

Two types of Values are used to indicate font-families of a document: family-name and generic-name. Examples of family-names are: Times, Arial, and Garamond. Family-names of more than one word should be enclosed in quotes; e.g., "New Century Schoolbook." Generic-names are less specific, indicating a major characteristic of a font-family. Accepted Values are: `serif`, `sans-serif`, `monospace`, `cursive`, and `fantasy`. Very often, more than one font-family will be specified for an element such that the browser has an ordered choice of names to use depending on what is available on the given platform. In the source code, for instance, the `BODY` style lists three font-families: `Arial`, `Helvetica`, and `sans-serif`. This allows the browser to work through the list of choices until it finds a family it is able to display; if none of the choices are possible, the browser will use its own default font.

`font-style`   Sets the display of a font to either oblique or italic.

Note the difference in the display of oblique text in Figures 10.3 and 10.4. Netscape 4.06 renders the style normally and, while it still isn't exactly right, Internet Explorer 5.00 renders it as italic.

`font-weight`   Sets the heaviness of a font.

The values of `font-weight` will produce different results depending on the font-family selected. While "`normal`" and `400` both mean the default font-weight, the actual appearance may differ drastically. The relative Values of weight (as in relative to the last weight set) are `bold`, `bolder`, and `lighter`. The absolute Values, lightest to heaviest, are `100, 200, 300, ..., 900`.

`font-size`   Sets the size of a font.

Size may be set with four styles of the following Values:

Absolute—Based on the font-sizes set in the browser's style sheets. The accepted Values are: `xx-small`, `x-small`, `small`, `medium` (the default size for a font-family), `large`, `x-large`, and `xx-large`.

Relative—Size is rendered relative to the absolute size of the parent element. Note how the paragraph, which is a child element of the body, is shown with slightly smaller than usual text in Figure 10.3. Note as well that Explorer does not register any difference. Values for `font-size` are: `medium`, `smaller`, and `larger`.

Length—Size is expressed as absolute Values such as `points`, `millimeters`, `inches`, etc.

Percentage—Size is expressed as a percentage of the parent font size.

`text-decoration`   Adds underlining, overlining, strike-out, or blink to text. Accepted Values are: `none`, `overline`, `underline`, `line-through`, and `blink`. Again, notice the differences in how Netscape and Explorer handle the attribute's Values.

`text-transform`   Changes the case of text.

The Values of `text-transform` tell the browser how to display the text within an element. Figures 10.3 and 10.4 show the paragraph rendered with the value **capitalize,** which causes the first letter of each word to be capitalized. `upper` will transform an element's text content to all upper-case, and `lower` to all lower-case.

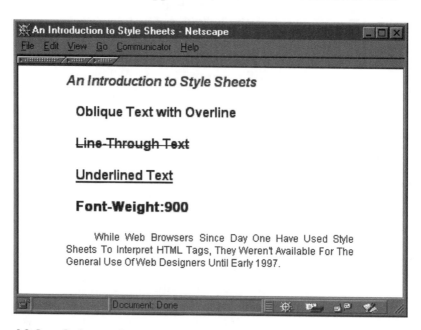

Figure 10.3 ■ Selected text properties rendered by Netscape 4.06.

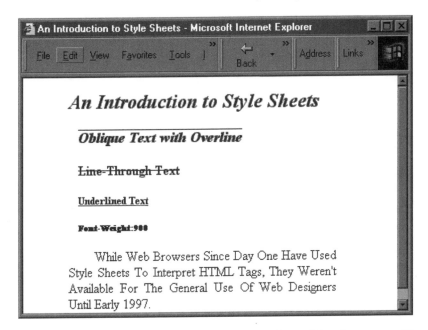

Figure 10.4 ■ Selected text properties rendered by Internet Explorer 5.00.

LAB 10.3 EXERCISES

10.3.1 BASIC STYLE PROPERTIES AND VALUES

a) Write a rule to present a paragraph's text as all blue caps in the Helvetica font.

_____

_____

b) Write an H3 rule that tells the browser to work through three fonts: Times Roman, New Century Schoolbook, and Century Gothic, until it finds a font it can display. Have the browser default to any serif font if none of the others are available.

_____

_____

c) Write the code to incorporate an external style sheet named `mystyle.css` into an HTML file.

LAB 10.3 EXERCISE ANSWERS

10.3.1 ANSWERS

a) Write a rule to present a paragraph's text as all blue caps in the Helvetica font.

Answer:
```
P {color:blue;
      text-transform:upper;
      font-family:Helvetica
   }
```

b) Write an H3 rule that tells the browser to work through three fonts: Times Roman, New Century Schoolbook, and Century Gothic, until it finds a font it can display. Have the browser default to any serif font if none of the others are available.

Answer:
```
H3 {font-family:"Times Roman", "New Century
      Schoolbook", "Century Gothic", serif
      }
```

c) Write the code to incorporate an external style sheet named `mystyle.css` into an HTML file.

Answer:
```
<HEAD>
    <LINK REL=STYLESHEET TYPE="text/css"
    HREF="mystyle.css"
    </HEAD>
```

LAB 10.3 SELF-REVIEW QUESTIONS

1) Only one font may be specified for a single selector.
   a) True
   b) False

2) Style rules in an external style sheet will be overridden by rules that are included in an HTML file.
   a) True
   b) False

3) The `capitalize` Value for the `text-transform` Property causes text to be rendered in all caps.
   a) True
   b) False

4) Which of the following is considered to be a generic font-family name?
   a) Helvetica
   b) Arial
   c) Sans-serif
   d) All of the above
   e) None of the above

Quiz answers appear in the Appendix, Section 10.3.

LAB
10.3

L A B   1 0 . 4

SPACE PROPERTIES AND VALUES

SPACE PROPERTIES

The source code for the styles rendered in Figures 10.7 and 10.8 is:

```
<HTML>
<HEAD>
<TITLE>An Introduction to Style Sheets</TITLE>
<STYLE>
BODY {background-color:#ffffff;
     color:#000000;
     margin-left:8%;
     font-family:Arial, Helvetica, sans-serif
     }

P    {text-indent:2em;
     margin-left:10%;
     margin-right:10%;
     padding:2em;
     border-color:red;
     border-style:groove;
     border-width:thick;
     text-align:justify;
     text-transform:capitalize;
     line-height:16pt
     }

</STYLE>
</HEAD>
```

`margin`	Sets the space between an outside edge and an element's contents. A margin may be set as a percentage of the element's actual size or as an absolute,

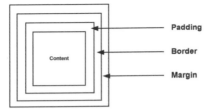

Figure 10.5 ■ An element's margin, border, and padding illustrated.

e.g., 2em. Interesting effects can be achieved by setting a margin to a negative number, but this should be done with care. See Figures 10.10 and 10.11 for examples of how Netscape and Internet Explorer display the same negative margin. The four parts of an element's margin may be set individually using the `margin-top`, `margin-right`, `margin-bottom`, and `margin-left` Properties. See Figure 10.5 for an illustration of an element's margin, border, and padding.

**LAB
10.4**

`border-color` Sets the color of an element's border. It is difficult to see in a black and white figure, but in ours, Netscape 4.06 is able to display a red border-color and Explorer 5.00 is not.

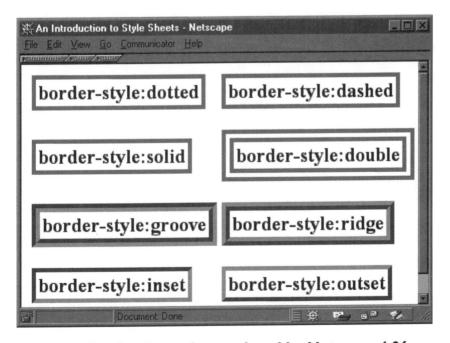

Figure 10.6 ■ Border styles rendered by Netscape 4.06.

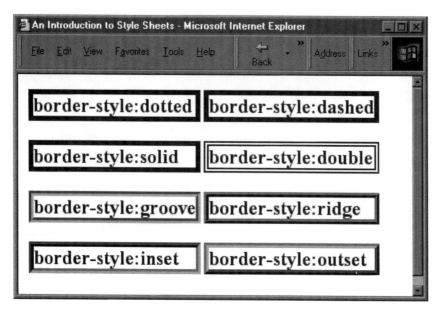

Figure 10.7 ■ Border styles rendered by Internet Explorer 5.00.

border-style	Sets the appearance of an element's border. The nine accepted Values, not including **none** are shown in Figures 10.6 and 10.7.
	Note how neither browser is able to interpret dotted and dashed borders as one might expect.
border-width	Sets the thickness of an element's border.
	Relative Values for border-width, which depend on the browser, are thin, medium (the default when a border-width is not specified), and thick. Absolute width Values may also be specified as points, ems, pixels, or millimeters. Finally, the border-width may be set as a percentage of the parent element's width.
padding	Sets the width of space between an element's content and its border. Padding Values may be expressed as a percentage of the parent element's width or in absolute lengths (points, pixels, ems, millimeters).
text-align	Sets the text alignment for an element. Allowed Values are left, right, center, and justify.
text-indent	Indents the first line of an element's text. The Value of the Property can be expressed as a length or a percentage of the element's width. It should be noted that the Value can be a negative length, which allows the Web author to create hanging paragraphs.

`line-height`   Sets the height of a line of text, or how far apart lines are in a block of text. The Value of `line-height` can be a length, a percentage of the current `font-size`, or a point size.

Now that you have learned the details of a number of space Properties and their Values, re-examine the code at the beginning of this section and observe the differences in how the styles are rendered by Netscape and Internet Explorer (Figures 10.8 and 10.9).

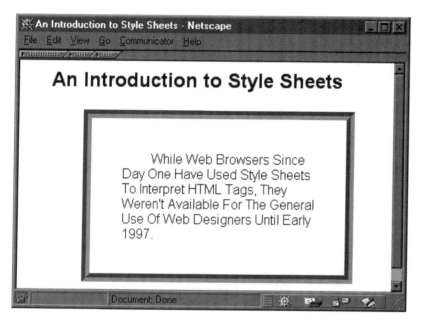

Figure 10.8 ■ Selected space properties rendered by Netscape 4.06.

**LAB
10.4**

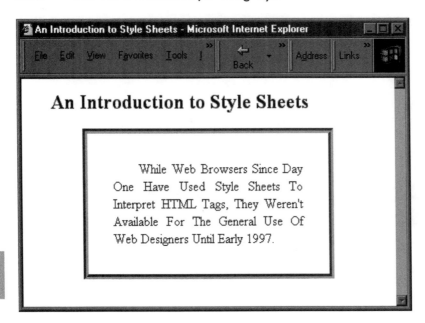

**LAB
10.4**

Figure 10.9 ■ Selected space properties rendered by Internet Explorer 5.00.

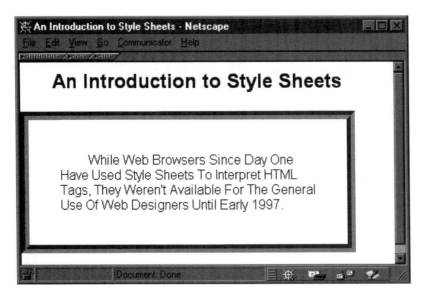

Figure 10.10 ■ A negative margin rendered by Netscape 4.06.

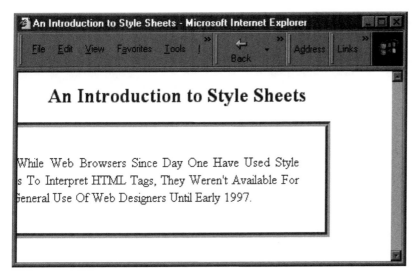

Figure 10.11 ■ A negative margin rendered by Internet Explorer 5.00.

LAB 10.4 EXERCISES

10.4.1 GUIDELINES FOR USING STYLE

a) Write the rule to render H1 with a medium-width border, a margin of 10 pixels, and a padding of 15 pixels.

_____

_____

b) Write the code to create paragraphs with all but the first line indented 5 pixels.

_____

_____

c) Write a rule to render text within the body of a document as 10 pt Arial font with the line height set to 120% of the font size.

_____

_____

10.4 EXERCISE ANSWERS

10.4.1 ANSWERS

a) Write the rule to render H1 with a medium-width border, a margin of 10 pixels, and a padding of 15 pixels.

Answer:
```
H2 {border-width:medium;
    margin:10px;
    padding:15px
    }
```

b) Write the code to create paragraphs with all but the first line indented 5 pixels.

Answer: `P {text-indent:-5px}`

c) Write a rule to render text within the body of a document as 10 pt Arial font with the line height set to 120% of the font size.

Answer:
```
BODY {font-family:Arial;
      font-size:12pt;
      line-height:120%
      }
```

LAB 10.4 SELF-REVIEW QUESTIONS

1) A margin is
   a) The space between an element's content and the outside edge
   b) The space between an element's content and the border
   c) The space between a border and the outside edge

2) The `text-indent` Property, when set,
   a) Indents all the lines of an element
   b) Indents the first line of an element

3) The `line-height` Property is used to set
   a) The size of the font within a line
   b) The height of a line

4) Margins and `text-indents` may have negative Values.
   a) True
   b) False

Quiz answers appear in the Appendix, Section 10.4.

C H A P T E R   1 0

TEST YOUR THINKING

The projects in this section use the skills you've acquired in this chapter. The answers to these projects are available to instructors only through a Prentice Hall sales representative and are intended to be used in classroom discussion and assessment.

Return to the pages you have created for your Web site and think about how you would logically incorporate style sheets into your work. Are there font and formatting characteristics that are used uniformly throughout your site that might be rewritten into an external style sheet that can be used by all of your pages? Create a single style sheet and link to it from several of your pages.

1) Create a single style sheet to be used as the default style for your Web site. Use the sheet set fonts, margins, and text colors.

2) Override the external style sheet by adding style to the HEAD of several documents.

3) Override the HEAD in a few selected elements.

A P P E N D I X

ANSWERS
TO SELF-REVIEW
QUESTIONS

CHAPTER 1
Exercise 1.1 ■ Self-Review Answers

Question	Answer	Comments
1)	c	Choice a is a proper name and c is a recognizable address.
2)	c	A "good" password should be a combination of special characters, numbers, and upper and lower case letters.
3)	c	Images and compiled programs are examples of binary files.
4)	b	The integrity of a password should be protected by changing it periodically.

Exercise 1.2 ■ Self-Review Answers

Question	Answer	Comments
1)	c	A directory name will normally be followed by a '/'
2)	c	ls lists all normal file and directory names within a given directory.
3)	d	ls -alg lists file and directory names, dot file names, and detailed information about the directory's contents.
4)	b	Remember, in UNIX "No news, is good news."

Exercise 1.3 ■ Self-Review Answers

Question	Answer	Comments
1)	a	UNIX is case sensitive.
2)	b	rmdir alone will only work with empty directories.
3)	b	UNIX will, by default, overwrite files without any forewarning.

4)	b	UNIX, by default, will not ask for any confirmation prior to deleting files.
5)	b	The command `rm -r` will remove a directory and all of its contents recursively.
6)	b	Again, UNIX is case sensitive. `PARROTS` and `parrots` would be the names of two completely distinct files.

Exercise 1.4 ■ Self-Review Answers

Question	Answer	Comments
1)	a	read=4, write=2, execute=1
2)	b	read=4, execute=1
3)	c	Web browsable files should be readable by the world.
4)	c	The x permission makes a file to be executed and a directory to be entered.

CHAPTER 2
Exercise 2.2 ■ Self-Review Answers

Question	Answer	Comments
1)	b	It is, in fact, important to check your Web pages using as many different browsers on as many different platforms as possible.
2)	c	High speed lines are still used mostly by the business world and a Web author should keep this in mind when designing pages.
3)	d	A careful analysis of a Web site's intended audience will affect nearly all aspects of the site if the results are applied.

Exercise 2.4 ■ Self-Review Answers

Question	Answer	Comments
1)	b	While links should make site navigation easy, they should also make sense.
2)	b	The point is to link to sites that are relevant to your subject in a strategically sensible manner.
3)	a	Strategically planned links can help to guide visitors through a Web site in a logical fashion.

Exercise 2.5 ■ Self-Review Answers

Question	Answer	Comments
1)	b	For larger sites it may make perfect sense to use different page layouts for different areas.
2)	c	Because the way the western world eye naturally starts at the top left corner of a page.

3)
    Relevance
    Accuracy
    Timeliness
    Spelling & Grammar
    Originality
    Give Something Away

CHAPTER 3
Exercise 3.1 ■ Self-Review Answers

Question	Answer	Comments
1)	a	HTML should not be referred to as a programming language. It is a means of marking up content in order to suggest presentation.
2)	b	Older browsers may not be able to interpret the latest HTML elements.

Exercise 3.5 ■ Self-Review Answers

Question	Answer	Comments
1)	b	The point of neat, easily readable HTML files is to make them accessible to the human being.
2)	b	While it will not be rendered as part of a Web page by the browser, the content of the TITLE tag is saved when a visitor bookmarks a page.
3)	b	Comments may appear anywhere in an HTML document and should be used liberally.

Exercise 3.6 ■ Self-Review Answers

Question	Answer	Comments
1)	b	The Paragraph element inserts space between paragraphs.
2)	b	Browsers will ignore the occurrence of multiple Paragraph elements.
3)	a	The http attribute will link the visitor to another Web page
	b	ftp will start a file download process
	c	mailto allows the visitor to send email using his default mail program
4)	c	The ALT attribute is used to provide text content to be rendered by browsers that do not display images. The newer browsers display this text when the mouse pointer is placed on an image.
5)	c	By default the ALT attribute may contain up to 1024 characters.
6)	b	Alternate text is not *required* for your Web pages to be rendered by a browser, but they should be included for all images.

CHAPTER 4
Exercise 4.2 ■ Self-Review Answers

Question	Answer	Comments
1)	b	Inline elements do not break to a new line.
2)	a	Block level elements will break to a new line.
3)		Identify the following as Block-level, Inline, or Invisible elements.

	Block-Level	Inline	Invisible
<!--			_X_
A		_X_	
DD	_X_		
DL	_X_		
EM		_X_	
H1 – H6	_X_		
HEAD			_X_
I		_X_	
IMG		_X_	
LI	_X_		
OL	_X_		
P	_X_		
PRE	_X_		
STRONG		_X_	
TITLE			_X_
UL	_X_		

4)	b	Content-base elements indicate that text should be rendered differently from surrounding text
5)	a	Physical elements dictate the appearance of content.
6)		Identify the following elements as either physical or content-based:

	Physical	Content-based
SMALL	_X_	
CITE		_X_
TT	_X_	
BLINK	_X_	
BIG	_X_	
I	_X_	
EM		_X_

SUP	_X_	____
B	_X_	____
PRE	_X_	____
STRONG	____	_X_
CODE	_X_	____
SUB	_X_	____

Exercise 4.3 ■ Self-Review Answers

Question	Answer	Comments
1)	a	The HREF address is a complete URL
2)	b	The HREF address is relative to the location of the current page.
3)	b	# refers to a labeled section within an HTML page.
4)	c	
5)	b	Links should be used judiciously to enhance the information being presented.
6)	b	Link lists are overused and often cumbersome. Use them sparingly.

Exercise 4.4 ■ Self-Review Answers

Question	Answer	Comments
1)	c	In an ordered list, the order of the list items, by default, matters.
2)	c	Unordered list items are preceded by bullets.
3)	a	The disc is the default bullet for unordered lists.
4)	c	The list will start at thirteen as "m" is the thirteenth letter of the alphabet.

Exercise 4.5 ■ Self-Review Answers

Question	Answer	Comments
1)	b	The default margin for an image is two pixels and is often enlarged to increase the ease of reading text when it flows around an image.
2)	a	An image is an inline element.
3)	c	The top value of the align attribute aligns the top of an image with a single line of text.
4)	c	The left value of the align attribute aligns the image to the left and flows text around it.
5)	b	The vspace attribute is used to adjust the top and bottom margins of an image.
6)	a	Image buttons will have borders by default and in many cases this is the only way your visitor will know an image is a link to another page of content.

Exercise 4.6 ■ Self-Review Answers

Question	Answer	Comments
1)	b	Colors may display differently on different platforms using different browsers. It is in your best interest to verify that your colors appear as you expect them to by using as many platforms and browsers as possible.
2)	b	The hexadecimal or RGB values of colors are more widely understood by browsers.
3)	c	Tiling can be an interesting effect at times, but more often than not will make text difficult to read.
4)	c	When setting the background color of a page, one should **always** set the text color.
5)	a	This is why text and background colors should always be set together for a Web page.
6)	d	Background images should be used carefully.

CHAPTER 5
Exercise 5.2 ■ Self-Review Answers

Question	Answer	Comments
1)	b	The browser will render a table as large as it needs to display all of the contents.
2)	a	By default, tables align to the left and external text will appear above and below it.
3)	b	Tables were originally conceived as a means of presenting tabular data in a more sophisticated manner than was previously possible with the PRE element.

Exercise 5.3 ■ Self-Review Answers

Question	Answer	Comments
1)	e	Table data cells may contain almost any HTML element, including other tables.
2)	b	The width and height of data cells will adjusted to accommodate the content by default.
3)	a	The browser will override height and width specifications if it needs more space to display content.
4)	b	The width of a cell can be set to a number columns.
5)	b	Captions default to the top center of a table and can be re-aligned using the align attribute.
6)	a	A table's width can be set to more than 100% of the browser window's width.
7)	b	Cellpadding is often increased from its default value of one pixel to improve the readability of content.
8)	d	Background colors can be varied within a single table but this should be done with care so as not to detract from the readability of the table data.

Exercise 5.5 ■ Self-Review Answers

Question	Answer	Comments
1)	c	A nested table appears within a cell of another table.

CHAPTER 6
Exercise 6.2 ■ Self-Review Answers

Question	Answer	Comments
1)	b	Frames should be used carefully so as not to completely overwhelm the visitor with too much information at once.
2)	b	While most of the newer browsers are frames capable the older browsers (some of which are still in use) are not.
3)	b	The NOFRAMES element is used to provide alternative text to be displayed by browsers that cannot render frames.
4)	a	Sizing your frames in percentages allows the browser to render the page to fit its window.
5)	c	A four window frame page, assuming each window displays a unique HTML page, will require five HTML files.
6)	b	Scroll bars will not appear by default if no scrolling is required.
7)	b	The NORESIZE attribute prevents the visitor from resizing frame windows.

Exercise 6.3 ■ Self-Review Answers

Question	Answer	Comments
1)	b	Nested frames are framesets within framesets.

CHAPTER 7
Exercise 7.2 ■ Self-Review Answers

Question	Answer	Comments
1)	b	Think of car radios here. It is possible to select only one button, or radio station, at a time.
2)	b	The SIZE attribute specifies the length of text field to be displayed on the form page. MAXLENGTH is used to set the maximum length allowed for the entry.
3)	d	The VALUE attribute is used to assign the text submitted when radio buttons and checkboxes are selected, the default value for text fields, and text labels on submit and reset buttons.
4)	a	Checkboxes, unlike radio buttons, allow the visitor to select more than one item in a list.
5)	b	The ROWS and COLS attributes set the size of a displayed textarea.
6)	c	The SELECT attribute is used to create both scrolling and pulldown menus.
7)	a	SIZE, when specified, creates a scrolling menu.

CHAPTER 8
Exercise 8.1 ■ Self-Review Answers

Question	Answer	Comments
1)	b	Server Side Includes are processed by the host machine. Because of this additional use of system resources they are not always permitted on public Web servers.
2)	a	An ISP may decide that SSIs use too much of a machine's available resources and decide not to offer the functionality.
3)	b	The source code viewed via a browser will contain the results of SSI processing, not the SSI code.
4)	d	Depending on what is allowed by the server hosting your pages, SSIs can be used to display system information, execute UNIX commands, and include external files in the current document.

Exercise 8.2 ■ Self-Review Answers

Question	Answer	Comments
1)	b	The environment variables discussed in this chapter are native to UNIX Operating Systems.
2)	b	Consult your ISP's system information to find out which environment variables are available on their servers.
3)	c	For instance: <!--echo var="HTTP_USER_AGENT"-->
4)	d	Config can be used to format date output.
5)	b	DATE_LOCAL displays current date and time at the Web site's location.

Exercise 8.4 ■ Self-Review Answers

Question	Answer	Comments
1)	c	Depending on how a server is set up, some, all, or none of the UNIX command set may be available for execution via SSIs.
2)	a	Inclusion of HTML, HEAD, TITLE, and BODY elements in files that are to be included in other files via SSIs may cause browser interpretation errors.
3)	b	Included files may contain additional SSIs.

Exercise 8.5 ■ Self-Review Answers

Question	Answer	Comments
1)	a	Wild cards allow for more generic testing.
2)	b	Multiple environment variables can be tested to determine how to proceed.
3)	a	SSIs can be used to restrict access to Web pages but should not be viewed as any sort of ultimate security.
4)	a	&& (and) and || (or) can be used to test more than one condition at a time.

CHAPTER 9
Exercise 9.2 ■ Self-Review Answers

Question	Answer	Comments
1)	a	The name of the file containing access instructions is called .htaccess.
2)	b	.htaccess' directives only apply to the contents of the directory in which it resides.
3)	c	The directive denies access to anyone from the arlyn.com domain.
4)	b	A user who has been denied access to a Web page will receive an Error 403 page.

Exercise 9.4 ■ Self-Review Answers

Question	Answer	Comments
1)	b	Password protection should never be considered absolute security.
2)	b	While passwords created by htpasswd are encrypted, it is not a good idea for password files to be browseable via the Web.
3)	b	.htaccess is used to password protect directories.
4)	b	Manually edit a password file to remove a user id and password.

CHAPTER 10
Exercise 10.1 ■ Self-Review Answers

Question	Answer	Comments
1)	b	Style sheets have long been used by the browsers. It was in 1997 that they were finally made available to Web designers.
2)	c	Semi-colons separate multiple declarations.
3)	b	Colons separate properties and values.
4)	b	Interpretation of style sheets varies widely between browsers.

Exercise 10.3 ■ Self-Review Answers

Question	Answer	Comments
1)	b	Multiple fonts may be specified for a single selector, but the browser will render the the first choice it has available.
2)	a	Browsers, most often, will follow the most "recent" style rule.
3)	b	The capitalize value causes the first letter of each word in an element to be capitalized.
4)	c	Helvetica and Arial are members of the sans-serif font-family.

Exercise 10.4 ■ Self-Review Answers

Question	Answer	Comments
1)	a	The margin is the space between an element's content and its outside edge.
2)	b	The text-indent property indents the first line of an element's text.
3)	b	The line-height property sets the height of a line containing text but does not affect the size of the text itself.
4)	a	Margins and indents may have negative values, but should be set with care as the browsers vary in their rendering of a negative value.

INDEX